Royal Recollections
Stories of Travel, Royalty & Collecting

Andrew Lannerd

Front cover photograph: Andrew Lannerd aboard the *Queen Mary 2*, November 2019.

Copyright © Andrew Lannerd, 2021.

First published in Great Britain in 2021.

The right of Andrew Lannerd to be identified as author of this work has been asserted by him in accordance with the Copyright, Designs and Patents Act 1988.

All rights reserved. No portion of this book may be reproduced in any form without written permission from the Author, except as permitted by U.K. or U.S. copyright law. For permissions contact: alannerd@transcendent-travel.com.

Cover design by Stephanie Derybowski.

Also available as a Kindle eBook.

www.transcendent-travel.com

Contents

Page 4 | Introduction

Page 7 | Chapter One: Dreams for The Future

Page 17 | Chapter Two: The Show Must Go On!

Page 31 | Chapter Three: Royal Encounters

Page 53 | Chapter Four: The Makings of a Company

Page 69 | Chapter Five: Collecting

Page 82 | Chapter Six: A Tale of Two Weddings

Page 95 | Chapter Seven: "The World is Your Oyster"

Page 115 | Chapter Eight: "You're Still Here!"

Page 127 | Chapter Nine: Pursuing the Object

Page 135 | Chapter Ten: Windsor Park to Windsor

Page 143 | Acknowledgements

Introduction

> "To move, to breathe, to fly, to float,
> To gain all while you give,
> To roam the roads of lands remote,
> To travel is to live."

…as the prolific writer Hans Christian Anderson famously wrote.

His passage reads like a personal invitation.

Travel and unique experiences represent life to me, and I've known this since I was young. Looking at my surroundings growing up in a small town in the United States, I kept asking myself: "Isn't there something more?"

I have been on a lifelong quest to answer that question.

Having a dream is rarely enough. Acting on a dream takes resolve, resourcefulness, and resources. My story is no exception. Before I was of the age and means to explore the world on planes and trains, I travelled the world through the pages of history.

History is, by definition, retrospect. And in retrospect, two dates became the catalyst to alter the events of my life. The first was on 31 August 1997 and the days following the death of Diana, Princess of Wales. The second took place on 21 September 2001, the first time I set foot on English soil.

In today's world a sense of occasion is easily lost. There is a tendency to wait "until I am older" or wait until "I have the right person to experience something with", or we delay things until that "special occasion" comes along.

Why do we limit ourselves? None of us can be promised tomorrow, yet we save the special china for only once a year. Every day is a gift, and life can be special, magnificent, and beautiful - with a little effort.

We've all heard of a person like my close friend, who invested everything she could into her retirement. She often spoke with enthusiasm, dreaming about how she hoped to travel the world down the line. For her adventures of travel were something to be earned. She always planned to make that trip "one day". Shockingly, she passed away before *that* day ever came.

Witnessing and being close to situations such as these cause us to re-examine our own mortality and reassess how we choose to live each day. I believe that *now* is the time, and that chosen way of living has led to some very interesting and rewarding experiences.

So begins the story of how a boy from Indiana had the dream at a young age to do more and to be more. Mine is the story of following a dream, the challenging task of building a business, and of a strong resolve to live rather than merely to exist.

Along the way, there have been discoveries, disappointments, and delights, each enriching in innumerable ways.

I invite you to join me on a journey where I'll guide you from encounters with royalty to exotic destinations, as well as share tales from tours and the determination of a collector.

Those who know me best will never say I lack passion. The stories you are about to read are the result of this passion, and I hope they inspire you to pursue your own.

Andrew Lannerd
Summer 2020

Chapter One:
Dreams for The Future

"Come on, Andrew! Aren't you going to play?" I looked at them covered in mud from head to toe. My reply at the age of 10 would likely be the same today, "Thank you, but I don't play in mud."

Looking back to my childhood, I knew I was different than those around me. Most children (especially other boys) were interested in video games and athletics, while I was interested in history, maps, geography, and collecting.

Even then, as today, my interests bordered on the eccentric, and the people I was drawn to tended to be much older than me. I always found older people more interesting. I would listen with enthusiasm to their stories, outlook, and life experiences. I found it easy to talk with adults, and from as young as I can remember the concept of travel was of great interest.

Dreaming of travel was the escapism I needed growing up in rural Indiana. The closest town was 5 miles away. My father worked in Indianapolis, which was an hour's drive, while my mother never worked outside of the home. My two older sisters often teased me for my love of geography and my constant study of our family's *World Book* encyclopaedias. Even though my parents likely found my interests unusual, they did their best to encourage my love of history and geography.

We did some travelling when I was young. Usually to places like Williamsburg, Virginia; Asheville, North Carolina; or to Washington, D.C. These family vacations often centred around American historical places of distinction.

I enjoyed these early trips, however the more I studied American history, the more I became enthralled by the traditions and history not of the United States, but of Europe. It was, and is, grander and older, and has much more depth. On these vacations my interests were clearly leaning towards the old world.

First through serendipity then through choice, history, geography, and dreams of travelling became the outlets that I needed to feed my soul. And my soul needed to be fed. I needed to find my place of belonging. Instinctively I knew that was not rural Indiana, so I became determined to look out to the wider world, a place that I would eventually be allowed to explore.

This quest had to begin slowly so at the age of 12, I started my own local "department of tourism." Doesn't every child? I held open houses for family friends and would proudly display the latest travel brochures from around the world. I even had business cards printed, and as I built my own little tourist office the mailman frequently delivered more mail addressed to me than to my parents. Pamphlets on historical sites, museums, theme parks and so on, started to fill my room and I would spend hours combing through them learning what each area had to offer. I began to dream about the chance to go and see the places for myself.

I ordered the latest brochures from popular locations just in case a family friend wanted to do vacation research. Of course, that rarely happened, but I was prepared none the less to jump at the opportunity to loan my cherished guidebooks. As I looked at the various leaflets, I always wondered why one state would produce a glossy, fabulous travel catalogue while another would publish a flat, boring travel guide. Even then I was sizing up the competition in the travel market - something rather unusual for a 12-year-old, but it seemed completely normal to me.

Imagine the excitement as I rushed to and opened the mailbox each day to see what new guides had arrived for my ever-growing collection. *Collection* - now there is a word you will be seeing frequently throughout this book.

It may have started with travel brochures, yet even today I am a collector. When I was young, it was stamp collecting which evolved into what I called my very own, "memento museum." Within the "museum" there were objects acquired on vacations: Indian arrowheads, postage stamps, badges, souvenirs, and anything else I thought was special enough to be on display. I remember bringing friends into my room to see the various objects. There was such excitement talking about each piece, its history, and the place where I acquired it.

If you ask collectors when their passion started, almost always they will say it began in their early years, and that was certainly the case for me. As I accumulated the brochures and those many small objects, it gave rise to dreams about what I could become.

Back to those travel guides, which by now, were starting to stack up. Between the brochures and my budding knowledge of destinations around the world, surely there had to be a use for it all, but what was it? My knowledge was first used - perhaps tested - by my parents when, at the age of 13, I planned the family vacation to Virginia.

I mapped out the general outline of the trip, what we would see, as well as where we would stay. Yes, that was a lot of responsibility but I obviously made the grade. From that day forward I became our family's official vacation planner.

Also at the age of 13, another event happened that would change the course of my life. We all remember where we were when we heard about the car accident in Paris involving Diana, Princess of Wales.

I heard the news while talking to a friend on the telephone. "Did you hear what happened in Paris?" he said. At the time, from early reports it seemed as if Diana's injuries were minor. Later that evening it was announced that she had passed away. I remember thinking how sad and unfortunate, but really, how much did I know about her?

The most I knew at the time was that she had been married to Prince Charles, was young and had two sons around my age. It might surprise you to discover, that evening was not my first encounter (so to speak) with royalty.

In 1993, along with her two sons William and Harry, she had enjoyed a highly publicised trip to Walt Disney World in Florida. By coincidence my family and I were at the Magic Kingdom the very day Diana and her sons were visiting. Even though we didn't see them, most people in the park (including us) knew that they were there. In a way it was to be my first royal encounter, and a sign of what was to come.

Throughout the week of Diana's death I became fascinated with the ever-changing news and the way it evolved from day-to-day. Many were looking for someone to blame for the tragedy. Diana was only 36 years of age.

The press began to question why the Royal Standard (the flag bearing the arms of the British sovereign) was not at half-mast over Buckingham Palace. Since this was the beginning of my royal interest, I was curious and suspected there must be reasoning or protocol behind this decision. Fascinated, I started researching and quickly discovered that the standard was the only flag (at that time) that could fly over the palace. It was not flown at half-mast for anyone, not even for The Queen's father King George VI on the occasion of his death in 1952.

The Royal Standard flying over the palace signifies the presence of the monarch, and because there is always a monarch on the British throne no flag had ever been flown at half-mast over Buckingham Palace. So goes the old saying, "The King is dead. Long live the King." Certain major newspapers knew this to be the case, but they were eager to have the attention and pressure diverted onto something emotive. They rightly sensed that public anger was building on speculations of how their news-hungry actions, payments to the paparazzi, and eventual pursuit of her car in Paris played a role in Diana's untimely death.

Two other memories immediately come to mind when recalling that fateful week. First, I remember watching The Queen's live, televised broadcast. Her presence prompted me to sit up and listen as it felt like history in the making. The broadcast was instrumental in shifting the public mood from anger to understanding. In it, Her Majesty paid tribute to Diana and reminded the British public that not only was she their queen, but she was also dealing with the difficult situation in her other role as a grandmother. It proved to be an impossible situation to get right.

The royal family were at Balmoral Castle at the time for their annual summer stay. Had they brought William and Harry immediately to London they would have been forced to mourn in the public spotlight. The Scottish Highlands afforded them the space and environment to mourn in private before they had to face the public mourning that was to come in London surrounding the funeral. The Queen's priority was to look after her grandchildren, and according to William and Harry in recent years she did just that in a thoughtful and caring way, shielding them as they came to terms with the death of their mother.

Certain press outlets were keen to portray The Queen as an out of touch monarch. These headlines had one purpose - to turn the broad public criticism away from the press, onto the institution of the monarchy.

To understand the character of Queen Elizabeth II is to know that she is, by nature, a reserved person. Her position has shaped her character to be cautious about showing emotion in public. It simply is not her style, and how refreshing that is in an age when we all know *too much* about the innermost feelings of some in the public eye. The Queen is not a celebrity. She is a living symbol of the United Kingdom, the Commonwealth, and over 1,000 years of British history.

My other strong memory of that week is of waking up early in the morning to watch the funeral coverage. Who could forget the scenes of mourners lining the streets of London, followed by the service in Westminster Abbey? The flowers and the handwritten card on the coffin that read "Mummy" were especially moving. This was a poignant reminder of the effect this had on two young boys who had lost their beloved mother.

I didn't know this at the time, but my life would change because of what I observed and later learned from the events of that week. Following the funeral I started to read as much as I could about the royal family. I devoured biographies, researched at the local library, watched documentaries, and scooped up as much information as I could.

I was an avid stamp collector at the time and Royal Mail released a special set of stamps to celebrate the Golden Wedding Anniversary of The Queen and The Duke of Edinburgh. I had to have the set and when they arrived I immediately fell for the beauty of the images. One stamp featured the royal couple on their wedding day, while the other was a special anniversary picture taken by Lord Snowdon the celebrated photographer and ex-husband of Princess Margaret. This was to be my first piece of royal memorabilia and I still have the set to this day. It makes me smile when I think of how far my collection and interests have grown.

In November 1997, I remember seeing news reports about the restoration of Windsor Castle following the disastrous fire of 1992. The Prince of Wales was giving a tour of St. George's Hall and I was enraptured by the splendour that I was seeing on the television screen. I knew at that moment that I had to go and see Windsor Castle for myself.

All these moments led me towards what my life would eventually become. Over the years I continued to read, study, and research the royal family, as well as learn more about London and the wider United Kingdom.

Such was my enthusiasm that I convinced my parents that a trip to England was necessary in my pursuit of knowledge. I would frequently drop hints and find good deals on flights, hoping that eventually they would give in, and in the end they did. Once the green light was given, we set the dates and I started planning. This was truly my moment. At the age of 17 I would be able to visit the places I longed to see.

I planned every detail. The route we would travel, where we would stay, and what we would see each day. My parents provided me with a budget and the planning commenced. I still have the copy of my typed itinerary and smile when I see how detailed it was. Small things were even included such as discounts at certain London restaurants for early dining and how to get from point A to point B. My passion for logistics started early.

At long last our departure day arrived: 20 September 2001 - yes, just a few days after the horrific events of 9/11 in the United States: 11 September 2001. As many will recall air travel stopped for days and it seemed as if our entire trip, the one I was so eager to take and in which I had invested so much, would not be possible. To my great relief the decision was made that, regardless of any travel concerns, we would proceed with the trip.

Our flight from Boston to London Heathrow was one of the first transatlantic flights that was permitted to depart. Imagine a huge airliner virtually empty. In our seating section there were, by count, more cabin crew than passengers.

The trip turned out to be everything I wished for and more. Imagine my excitement as I viewed the Houses of Parliament for the first time while crossing the River Thames by Westminster Bridge. Then I was awe-struck by the grandeur of the state apartments at Buckingham Palace, far more ornate and elaborate than any picture.

As we were about to leave Westminster Abbey the sound of the pipe organ began to fill the air. I turned to my parents and said, "Stop and listen. How often do you get to hear the organ play in Westminster Abbey?" Perhaps this was a moment of foreshadowing. Could unforgettable moments be curated?

Down the Thames in the Jewel House at the Tower of London, I amused everyone around us by repeatedly going round and round, over and over on the moving sidewalks that gently take visitors past the crown jewels. My eyes were ablaze with what I was finally seeing in person - St. Edward's Crown, the Sovereign's Sceptre with Cross, the Imperial State Crown, the Imperial Crown of India, and on and on. For me was a carousel of diamonds, rubies, and emeralds. After several circuits the point was clearly made that it was time to move on!

On a day trip to Windsor I marvelled at the majestic and ancient towers of Windsor Castle rising from the mist as we approached by train. It was a powerful moment. At the time I would never have imagined that years later Windsor would become my home, and the castle rising for nearly 1,000 years over the River Thames would be a sight that I would eventually enjoy on a daily basis.

Andrew, aged 17, at Windsor Castle.

In a way, I suspect that my parents thought this trip would be sufficient and that I would slowly move on to another passion. Nothing could have been further from the truth. Instead of the end of the interest, it was just the beginning.

The next few years would be defining ones in establishing a life-long passion.

Chapter Two:
The Show Must Go On!

"What is your dream job?" I replied without hesitation, "I want to plan unique tours of the UK."

Even at the age of 19, the word "unique" was something I knew needed to be explored when thinking about tours and travel in general. Anyone can take guests to the Tower of London, but I knew early on that there was more to curating an experience than simply admiring what you see. I eventually realised that behind-the-scenes access or special elements were the necessary ingredients. First, I had to discover these things for myself. Only then I could share them with others.

At 19 it was just a dream, and the fulfilment of that dream was still a few years and many sacrifices down the line. In the meantime, education was the priority, so I pursued a degree in Travel, Event and Hospitality Management - which felt tailor-made for me. My choice of degree was not a difficult decision. I knew early on that a career in the world of travel and event management was my preferred profession. Was it destiny? Destiny or not, I was certainly on an obvious path. And something stronger than accident was pushing me, or perhaps pulling me, in this direction.

Even though I longed to return to the UK during my education, I couldn't afford to do so at the time. Despite this I still found other ways to continue to pursue my interest in both the royal family and in Britain. The year 2002 stands out for the variety of major royal events that took place that year. In early February Princess Margaret, The Queen's sister, died at the age of 71.

In late March Queen Elizabeth The Queen Mother passed away, and there were enormous events that surrounded and followed her death. The Queen Mother was 101 years old at the time and was loved by the nation. Along with her husband King George VI she was a symbol of British resilience during the Second World War. During her lying-in-state in Westminster Hall (at the Houses of Parliament) an estimated 200,000 mourners filed past her coffin to pay their respects.

It was also the year of the Golden Jubilee of Her Majesty The Queen, marking her 50 years on the British throne. During this momentous summer The Queen undertook countless domestic and overseas tours, and celebrations were held both in the United Kingdom and around the Commonwealth.

From afar I watched these events with great interest, mounting enthusiasm, and a real sense of excitement. I still remember the hilarious moment when Dame Edna Everage introduced The Queen as, "The jubilee girl," in the gardens of Buckingham Palace! It was a summer to remember.

While I was disappointed that I couldn't travel to London to enjoy the many special events in 2002, I knew that The Queen would be in Ontario, Canada that October as part of her jubilee tour of Canada. I had to go. The possibility of seeing The Queen in person for the first time was of monumental significance to me. So how would I proceed? I had the budget of a college student, not to mention classes to attend, but I knew I *had* to make it happen.

My father offered to accompany me on the trip. I still wonder if it was to keep an eye on me, or to help pay for some of the costs. I suspect it was the latter. A family friend worked for an airline so I approached him to see if we could use two of his employee tickets to fly standby - which we did.

With the airfare arranged, next I approached my professors, which certainly created some apprehension on my part. Their refusal would make it difficult to proceed, yet I knew I could spin the idea to get the necessary approvals. I started with my program director and went down the line, asking each of my instructors, "Would it be possible for me to miss a couple days of classes?" I was a good student and most of them seemed to like me, so for me to ask they knew it had to be for something important. I continued, "Well, you see The Queen will be visiting Canada, so I'd really like to fly up and see her in person." A knowing smile often accompanied the approval for my request.

Being interviewed by the Canadian press, 10 October 2002.

This did not come as any great surprise since I was already well-known for my interest in all things British. Permission was granted with perhaps a little amusement and no doubt behind-the-scenes gossip aimed at my enthusiasm.

The day: The 10th of October 2002. The place: Sheridan College in Oakville, Ontario, just outside of Toronto. I was keen to be present for every single moment, so we travelled a day in advance.

We were the first members of the public to arrive at Sheridan College at 7:30 am, the day of the event. The Queen's visit was not scheduled until noon, but I was determined to have the best possible viewing position. As is the case with every royal visit the press also arrived in advance, along with others, who like me, were there to catch a glimpse. The crowd began to swell as the time came closer for the royal arrival.

When the press learned just how far my father and I had travelled we became the subject of their attention and I was interviewed several times throughout the day. My unique story was shared on television, the local radio station, and there was even a small write-up in the newspaper. As this was my first royal visit experience, the press interest was fun and added to the enjoyment of the day.

There is always a bit of excitement whenever The Queen is about to arrive. You can feel it in the air. The hush of a large crowd, the sound and sight of a motorcade, and then the car door opens. The anticipation is everywhere and then she appears. I recall cheering her. *How could you not?*

I am sure my boisterous greeting was over the top, but I remember well Her Majesty's smile in response as I celebrated her arrival. She was wearing a beautiful blue coat and hat, and I can still see her diamond brooch sparking in the autumn sunlight.

The excitement of seeing The Queen in person for the first time was certainly something I had to experience again. Although I didn't know it at the time the royal visit would become a familiar part of my life over the next few years.

The first photograph I took of The Queen in Oakville, Ontario, 10 October 2002.

When I returned and resumed my classes everyone was eager to hear stories and see pictures of my royal experience. It is more than likely that this trip instilled in me the concept of experience-based travel. Instead of travelling to see a specific site I was travelling to have an experience, to do something special and achieve something unique. This realisation would have lasting effects on my future.

***

After graduating from college I spent over ten eventful years working for arts organisations in Indianapolis. My first position at the Indiana State Museum involved planning events and managing the museum's daily internal and external event calendars. Working in a museum appealed to my budding curatorial side, and I loved chatting with the conservation team and curators about new projects or unique finds.

The museum's storage rooms were especially tempting, and I would sneak down whenever possible to marvel at the various objects tucked away. Imagine slowly opening a drawer and finding a large variety of Mastodon bones placed alongside a painting of Abraham Lincoln. This was just one of many drawers waiting to be explored.

Although I loved my job at the museum, it was an entry level position and the salary reflected that. Despite a limited budget it became a priority to travel to London at every opportunity. These first trips would continue to encourage my passion for all things British and royal, and I managed to visit Britain a few times each year throughout my 20s. By the time I was nearing age 30, I was travelling to England between five and eight times a year. Thank goodness for those $600.00 USD roundtrip flights that were available at the time!

My early trips were possible because I lived in a less-expensive apartment than others, refused to pay for things like parking (I always found a way around it), and didn't spend very much of my extra income - except on travel.

Travelling was the priority, and not just to Europe. I loved short, inexpensive, weekend trips and whenever possible New York City became my destination of choice. I was a frequent flyer on the Friday afternoon non-stop flight to LaGuardia. Upon arrival, I travelled on the M60 bus to 125th Street in Manhattan. Once at 125th Street and Lexington Avenue, I'd hop on a 4, 5 or 6 Train and make my way downtown.

I became a regular at a small hostel in Greenwich Village and would queue up for cheap Broadway tickets, often standing in the rear of the theatre. My days were spent in galleries and museums, and long walks exploring every corner of Central Park. Evenings were spent discovering small eateries in Hell's Kitchen, followed by the theatre and late nights at jazz, piano, and cabaret clubs. I packed it in.

Then late Sunday evening it was time to return to Indianapolis, just in time for work on Monday morning. It was exhilarating.

Between the roundtrip flight that was consistently $125.00 USD and the hostel that was $32.00 USD a night, these frequent excursions were certainly affordable. The weekends were adventuresome and culturally valuable. They even bordered on bohemian, however don't ask me to travel this way nowadays, my tastes have matured, just as I have. But it was such fun at the time.

My first big career break came as the result of a conversation with a colleague and friend one day at the Indiana State Museum. "Andrew, there is a position open with the Indianapolis Symphony Orchestra. You would be perfect for it. Let me introduce you to someone." While I loved working at the museum the possibility of managing concerts for a major symphony orchestra was too good to miss. So I applied.

For the next five years I was the House Manager for the Indianapolis Symphony Orchestra, and was in charge of the front of house logistics for 200 indoor and outdoor performances each year. Additionally, I supervised 65 part-time employees and dealt with countless situations surrounding performances. These included customer service scenarios and frequent medical issues. It was a great job for someone so young, and a huge responsibility.

The events I oversaw ranged in attendance from 500 to 10,000 or more guests. In a way we were an extension of the orchestra. When I look back I am proud of what we achieved during those years. As my staff would well-remember, my mantra was, "Everything we do off-stage surrounding a performance should complement the artistic excellence on-stage." It was an exciting time even during exhausting weeks when we had as many as eight performances.

I have always been a stickler for standards. The Indianapolis Colts (an American football team) frequently held games at the same time as our performances. When this happened I received pressure from my staff to have the game showing on the lobby televisions. I hated the idea. In my mind showing a football game in the lobby, after patrons had just listened to Bach should simply *not* be done. My to the point response was well-known, "When the Indianapolis Colts broadcast *our* performances in their stadium, I'll return the favour."

Dealing with large numbers of the public on a regular basis and overseeing audiences often brought about hilarious and occasionally stressful situations. But of course, I had to keep a straight face, and remain composed and professional, even though I often wanted to laugh.

I cringe when recall the lady seated in dress circle who decided a quiet movement of Beethoven was the best moment to slowly open and indulge in her bag of potato chips. And I will never forget the couple I discovered in a compromising position during Rachmaninoff. There was never a dull moment in my world of live classical performances.

Making the entire concert experience *perfect* was my primary goal. I will never forget an employee at the time saying, "Andrew, I made a mistake." He went on to confess that he asked a concert patron when her baby was due. You guessed it, she wasn't pregnant and began crying, while her partner berated my employee. This is a mistake that every man on earth knows not to make. However, even though this employee was in his 50s, he made the irreversible error so I was called in to solve a rather tricky situation. An apology, complimentary drinks, and upgraded seats did the trick. Since she was not with child, a large gin martini minimised her anger rather quickly.

Then there was the *Valentine's Day concert to remember*. I was about to open the theatre for a sold-out performance (1,700 guests), and a few minutes before it was time to open the doors I received a call to come backstage to speak with the artistic team. When I arrived I was told that _an anonymous famous artist_ was feeling ill and wanted to cancel the performance. Can you imagine the horror of ruining Valentine's Day for 1,700 people?! I knew full-well that my staff would take the brunt of the crowd's anger, and it was just too late to cancel. I stressed that somehow, someway _anonymous famous artist_ had to go on, even if the concert had to be shorter than planned.

Luckily that is exactly what happened and I can still imagine, very vividly, the angry mob that we would have faced if we hadn't brought the artist on stage - if only for a short time. Even after obtaining special medication, the artist sounded awful, yet the concert attendees seemed sympathetic as he attempted to put them in the mood for love.

There were also medical emergencies during performances. These are far more frequent than most people realise. During my time with the orchestra, I saw it all. From strokes to heart attacks, to people falling down the stairs - remaining calm and dealing with things in an efficient manner was the only option.

"Andrew there's a bat in the auditorium!", the usher exclaimed as she ran towards me. How unfortunate since a performance was taking place at that precise moment. From the rear of a full auditorium I watched the bat diving over the musician's heads, their faces looking up in horror as they played on. The audience gasped and snickered as quietly as they could, but with every dive the situation was getting worse. Luckily it was about time for the intermission and I ran backstage to discuss "bat removal" scenarios with the stagehands.

As we were discussing the situation a musician said to me in a rather aggressive manner, "Andrew how are you going to get that bat OUT of here!" I replied with a smile, "Well since I can't shoot it, I'm looking at other options right now." Luckily once the performance resumed the bat decided the fun was over and stopped harassing the musicians and our patrons. Much to my relief it hid itself in the far corner of the auditorium ceiling. Thank goodness for that.

Once or twice a month we had daytime concerts which greatly appealed to the local senior and retirement communities. During these concerts I stood in the lobby ready to quickly react and solve issues. It might be a patron dispute over who owned a specific walker, wheelchair, or cane (they all looked alike and there were many at these performances) or yet another ambulance run. I was impressed early on at the arrival speed of the paramedics once we called for them. I quickly discovered that they simply looked at our performance schedule and would park around the block during these times - just waiting for our call.

It was not all about emergencies of course. Each week it was marvellous to turn the audio speaker on in my office and hear some of the world's greatest musicians during the rehearsals. There is something magical about playing a role in a part of something as wonderful as a major symphony orchestra. I became enchanted with the glories of the music and marvelled in everything from Sergei Rachmaninoff to George Gershwin.

I was well-known in the organisation for my love of music composed by George Frideric Handel, and lobbied behind-the-scenes, always hoping the orchestra would perform his works more often. One day in a meeting our vice president announced, "Andrew will be pleased as we've scheduled *Handel's Messiah* for next season." Strangely, the Indianapolis Symphony Orchestra had not performed *The Messiah* in many years, which I could never understand. My persistence worked at last.

The celebrities certainly left their mark as well. I worked with everyone from Yo-Yo Ma to Kenny Rogers, Joshua Bell to Chris Botti, and everyone in between. Backstage there were oddities such as this or that in the dressing room, or instructions like, "No eye contact should be made unless _an anonymous famous artist_ is speaking directly to you." And there were certainly one or two diva moments.

Imagine being asked by Gladys Knight's assistant to hold a jacket over Gladys' head while walking her to the car, as she was not interested in seeing her fans waiting outside. I did as requested, despite the unease that it caused me. I was aware that we were greatly disappointing those that had waited a long time in the cold, hoping to see her.

On another evening of note I was asked to dinner with Florence Henderson (Mrs. Brady in *The Brady Bunch*) following her performance. She was charming and such fun. As we sat down and ordered drinks, the waitress asked everyone, including Florence, for their IDs. Luckily she found that to be amusing. We all did, as she was in her mid-70s at the time. Later that night she asked me and a couple of others to her hotel suite. She had an outrageous sense of humour and said to us, "Come on, let's all get into bed together and take a picture." Which we did amongst great laughter. She was mischievous, playful, and oh such fun. So yes, I guess you could say I went to bed with Mrs. Brady.

My time with the Indianapolis Symphony Orchestra opened my eyes to a much wider world that was just waiting to be explored. Luckily my position had a generous vacation allowance. I used it at every available opportunity to jet off to England and other places across Europe. These trips became more and more frequent, and in early 2006 a chance meeting in London would open new and exciting doors for me.

***

Whoever said, "It's all in who you know," was completely right. Imagine meeting someone and becoming fast friends, only to discover that he works in Buckingham Palace and is part of the Royal Household, a member of The Queen's staff. That is exactly what happened to me.

The invitations started coming. From a drinks party in the palace overlooking the Queen Victoria Memorial, to seats in The Queen's Box at the Royal Albert Hall, to finally an event on the 14th of June in 2006.

We all have days which we would love to re-live if we could. For me, 14th June 2006, would certainly be at the top of my list. The day would begin with a very special acquisition for my collection and would end with the most memorable of memorable evenings.

The day started at Christie's auction house on King Street in London for the second day of a highly anticipated sale of the collection of the late Princess Margaret, from her apartment at Kensington Palace. In the weeks leading up to the sale I devoured each page of the auction catalogues and was determined to walk away with something for my own collection.

The viewing days before the sale were a treat, as it was an opportunity to see and handle the wonderful objects. I did this with great enthusiasm. "Could I please see the small Fabergé clock?" and "May I look closely at lot 345?" Nothing was off limits and it was a unique opportunity to view the things that belonged to her, up close and personal.

To be in the room and bidding on the day of sale involved quite an approval process - providing banking details, passport, and credit card information. During the viewing as I marked out my lots of interest I was astonished at the low estimates. The logic behind this was the enticement of more bidders. "Oh, the estimate is only £200, I'll have a go!"

As I entered Christie's on the day of the auction the rooms were filled with enormous fresh flower displays, and the saleroom was packed with the great and good of London. I took a seat in the second row not far from the auctioneer. Nervously with my bidding number and catalogue in-hand, the sale began, and I couldn't believe what started to unfold. Right then I knew I quickly had to change my tactics.

When the first lot opens and the estimate is £1,000 and it sells for £13,200, you know it no longer is a question of what you like, it turns quickly into what you can actually bid on and win. I knew straightaway I had to fight hard and fast, since there was too much worldwide attention to obtain a bargain or even one of the items featuring Margaret's cypher. Something featuring her cypher was what I really wanted. These rare and personal monogrammed items would come years later, but for that day the fighting commenced.

Lot 303, estimate at £250, sells for £6,600. Lot 317, estimate at £200, sells for £13,200, and on and on it goes. Each time there looks to be a glimmer of hope I raise my paddle, and then back out when necessary. Then comes the lot where I am the top bidder, it's looking good, yes, almost there and the auctioneer says, "This must be the bargain of the sale," and quickly the bids began again, knocking me out of position.

Shortly after, the auctioneer looked me in the eye and noticed my frustration. Because I was near him this helped my success. He recognised the determination I had. I *would* win something. He *owed me one*, so when the hammer finally came down a few lots later, I had acquired two pieces of china from Princess Margaret's collection.

It was success at last, but a very close call since I was at the high end of my budget. As the sale went on, more and more people were getting desperate to obtain something so the bids were going even higher. With hindsight, I was lucky that my tactics of bidding hard at the beginning paid off in the end.

Being in the room that day was electric. Sitting near me was William Tallon (known famously as Backstairs Billy) who was the personal page to Queen Elizabeth The Queen Mother, as well as a few other well-known faces.

There were countless exciting moments throughout the sale, and this increased when the auctioneer announced, "A member of the royal family will be bidding on the next lot." The room started buzzing - did that mean we should *not* be bidding, or did it mean that we *should* be bidding even more?

It was a morning and afternoon to remember, and I walked out of Christie's that day treasure in hand, and my head held high. As if all that was not enough, I was eager to get moving. I had to prepare for a very special evening to celebrate a birthday - in the gardens of Buckingham Palace.

Chapter Three:
Royal Encounters

"*The gardens were bathed in an evening glow, while champagne and music continued to flow. The kiss by a prince for his mother The Queen, was spotted by me just out of the scene. It was apparent to all in attendance, that this would be a night for remembrance.*"
-Andrew Lannerd, the evening of 14 June 2006

"There's a party at the palace later this summer for The Queen's 80th birthday," said my friend who worked in the Royal Household. My reaction was, "Oh, how nice."

There was a momentary pause on the telephone then he said, "Would you like to attend?"

My reply was calm and composed, while inside I was jumping up and down! Would anyone in their right mind turn down that invitation? Could it *really* be possible that I was to be a guest at a private party to celebrate The Queen's *80th* birthday?

As the time for the event came closer the excitement began to build. This was to be the first exclusive event I would attend with members of the royal family present.

I learned that it would be held in the gardens of the palace, but not like the annual summer garden parties attended by thousands of guests. This specific, special evening would be smaller and more intimate. It was a private party to celebrate The Queen's momentous year.

Imagine my delight when the invitation arrived. I carefully opened the envelope. The beautiful invitation was something special - printed on a thick, gold embossed card. It read:

> *The Master of the Household is commanded by Her Majesty to invite*
> *Mr. Andrew Lannerd*
> *to a Summer Party*
> *to be given by The Queen and The Duke of Edinburgh*
> *in the Gardens of Buckingham Palace*
> *on Wednesday, 14 June 2006 at 7:30 p.m.*
> *to mark The Queen's 80th Birthday*

As soon as the invitation arrived I knew my moment had come. Various royal invitations were already in my collection, but they were always addressed to *others*. Here was one addressed to *me*. I was over the moon.

On the day of the big event, I left Christie's with Princess Margaret's china in-hand and headed back to my hotel to change. The evening was a black-tie occasion, so I was keen to make sure that I looked my best.

My friend had also invited me to a pre-event gathering on the Footman's Floor of the palace. Arriving together we entered the palace by using the side entrance, just off of Buckingham Palace Road. After checking in with security we walked along the back corridors of the palace. It looked and felt like being backstage at a theatre, or in the staff corridors of a large hotel. Long passageways lead from end-to-end with interesting signs reading, "Silver Pantry" and "Footman's Livery." There was even a Coutts & Co. cash machine (Coutts & Co. are the bankers of the royal family).

Before we joined the pre-event gathering, I was given a behind-the-scenes tour of the palace that included the famous Centre Room and the Chinese Corridor - areas which are normally off limits to the general public. I remember peeking through the curtains of the Centre Room doors that are used by the royal family as they walk onto the iconic palace balcony. Additionally, as we had to navigate from the front of the palace to return back up to the Footman's Floor, we used The Queen's lift, which is adjacent to her private apartments. She was in residence at the time, so you can imagine my excitement as we moved ever closer and then around Her Majesty's private apartments.

Once at the gathering on the Footman's Floor we enjoyed a pre-party drink and socialised with a few other guests. Most were like my friend, members of the Royal Household - palace footmen, under butlers, etc. From the party we were able to look down at the palace gardens. Enjoying our drinks we watched the hospitality teams making the final preparations for the evening.

It was all hugely exciting. I kept pinching myself to make sure it wasn't a dream. In five years, I had gone from a first-time visitor touring the state apartments to an invited guest at Buckingham Palace. As if the day hadn't already been good enough, it was time for the real event to begin.

When the time came for the party to begin we returned back to the ground floor of the palace, approaching via the Marble Hall and the Bow Room. The hall is lined by marble columns, statues of kings and queens, and a few of the finest paintings in the Royal Collection. Flanking the doors of the Bow Room are two of my favourite paintings, both by the German artist Franz Xaver Winterhalter. One is a state portrait of Queen Victoria and the other Prince Albert, her consort.

From the Bow Room we stepped out onto the lawn. It was one of the most beautiful summer evenings one could imagine - ideal temperatures, early evening sunshine, lengthening summer shadows, and a soft breeze. I soon spotted the official photographer (personal cameras were not permitted) and quickly went over to have a word with her, hoping to charm her at my request. I mentioned that if she, "happened to capture a photograph of me with The Queen," that it would mean so much to have that image. Likely seeing my enthusiasm, she kindly replied, "Let me see what I can do." It was a case of the age old, 'If you don't ask, you'll never know…'

We started to mingle and then, shortly after, noticed that members of the royal family had quietly joined the party. Because the event was held in the gardens each guest was given a hamper which contained our dinner for the evening. It was marked in gold: *EIIR 80th Birthday*. In hindsight, we probably should have tucked our hampers away as it was not ideal for carrying around and mingling at the party.

Just as I was about to find a spot to lay down the hamper I noticed The Duke of Edinburgh walking towards us. I quickly straightened myself up as he casually inquired, "Oh, I see you found your hamper. What's inside?" I explained and then said, "Oh, and many happy returns for your birthday last weekend sir." His 85th birthday had been just a few days earlier. "Not many, just one is enough," he replied in his typical, to the point manner.

Then I noticed that The Queen had arrived and she was in a lovely light green ensemble. She along with various members of the royal family began mingling. I observed The Duke of York a few feet away greeting his mother with the customary kiss on each cheek, a kiss of the hand, then a neck bow.

Throughout the night there was only one star - The Queen. As she approached us everyone in our semi-circle gave her a neck bow or a curtsy. She then said with a smile, "No more 'Happy Birthday.' Everyone keeps wishing me 'Happy Birthday.'" Realising that this was my moment I replied, "Well your majesty, I hope you don't mind, but I'd like to also add *my* best wishes for your birthday." She looked at me, smiled warmly, and said, "Well okay, but you're the last one."

Her Majesty The Queen and Andrew Lannerd, 14 June 2006.

Her reply amused us all. It was a moment to remember. Not only do I have the memory, but I also have a cherished photograph of the interaction. The photographer came through for me in the end.

The evening went on and as she mingled it was easy to observe where The Queen was at any given moment. How did I know? As she moved through the crowd she was greeted with deep curtsies. It was rather like a sophisticated version of the Mexican wave during a sporting event.

As is customary with royal events, members of the royal family tend to depart quietly, allowing their guests to relax a little. Once The Queen departed the disco started in the garden and to my amusement the first song the DJ played was *Dancing Queen* by ABBA. As we danced the night away, I thought to myself, "How could *any* day be better than this?"

My time at Buckingham Palace continued into the late hours. Little did I know that years later I would still be looking back fondly at that special day to remember.

The short conversation with The Queen at the party to celebrate her 80th birthday was not my first exchange with Her Majesty. It had taken place the year before during The Queen's visit to Bristol in 2005. I learned that she would be undertaking various engagements in the city that day, so naturally I wanted to be a part of it. I travelled on the train from London the evening before her arrival.

The next morning, I am standing in the spot that I hoped would be a prime position. The location was a primary school that was scheduled to be The Queen's first stop of the day. Having picked up a bouquet of flowers the previous evening, I hoped for an opportunity to present them to her at some point during the day. The presentation of flowers is a customary mark of respect that members of the public do at times when greeting The Queen.

As I waited in the cold the press began to arrive, perhaps a little amused, noticing me standing in the icy cold air, holding a bouquet of flowers *hours* before the royal arrival. As this was one of my first royal events, I had failed to dress properly for the elements. I am sure the flowers became as frozen as I was.

As the time came closer for The Queen's arrival a member of the Royal Household walked over to me and said, "Her Majesty is coming out shortly, and she will walk over to you and accept your flowers." Can you imagine my excitement? The weather was no longer on my mind!

Then it happened. The Queen walked over to me, accepted the flowers and said, "They're lovely flowers," to which I replied, "Good morning, Your Majesty." She must have heard my accent and inquired, "Where are you from?" I answered, "The United States, and I've come to Bristol just to see *you* today ma'am." Appearing pleased, she responded, "How kind, thank you very much," and then moved on.

With Her Majesty The Queen in Cambridge, 27 April 2011.

The experience of having that quick interaction with The Queen would only deepen my interest and fascination. Although this was a brief encounter, I discovered her human side and natural ability to put those in her presence at ease.

Pictured with a rather elegant "hat" in Nottingham, 13 June 2012.

As the next few years progressed my royal encounters became more and more frequent. From train trips to see The Queen on one of her many regional tours, to special services and occasions wherever possible.

In 2007, during The Queen's State Visit to the United States, I followed her tour from Richmond to Williamsburg, Virginia, and then eventually to Washington, D.C. My planning was done with precision, but to my great annoyance the US officials had no intentions whatsoever to allow anyone from the general public to *actually* see her in-person.

Her visit to Richmond started with a "walkabout" on the lawn of the Virginia State Capitol. A royal walkabout is typically a chance for members of the public to see and potentially interact with a member of the royal family. These walkabouts were first introduced by The Queen in the 1970s during a tour of Australia and New Zealand.

I was delighted when a royal visit which included a "walkabout" was scheduled and announced for Richmond, only to find that day, the "walkabout" was only for invited guests of the Governor of Virginia. Members of the public, like myself, were kept far away.

Despite this setback I soldiered on with the tour and managed to catch brief glimpses of The Queen in Williamsburg, and later in Washington, D.C.

The Queen in Cambridge, 27 April 2011 (Photograph by Andrew Lannerd).

Over the years I have been present for The Queen's awayday visits, as Her Majesty's regional tours are called. I've travelled to see her at Stafford, Liverpool, Margate, Chester, Sheffield, Cambridge and Nottingham – just to name a few. I have been present for Royal Maundy services, Easter Sundays at Windsor Castle, Christmas days at Sandringham, Order of the Garter Services at Windsor, Holyrood Week in Edinburgh (when The Queen is officially in residence in Scotland), Remembrance Sunday commemorations at the Cenotaph, and at other royal visits and tours at every available opportunity.

The royal schedule is typically published a few months in advance, allowing me to make plans to observe the royal visits. Occasionally however, there have been random royal encounters, which can be unexpected and fun. I remember sharing a tube journey with Princess Anne's husband, Vice Admiral Sir Timothy Lawrence, and discovering that The Duchess of Kent was also a guest in the same small Suffolk hotel where I was staying.

One day as I sipped my drink at a favourite venue in London, the familiar face of Jack Brooksbank (Princess Eugenie's husband) walked in. My friend and I noticed and said, "Wouldn't it be fun if Princess Eugenie came in," and less than ten seconds later she did. In these instances, members of the royal family are entitled to their privacy, so from a distance, I merely sneak an appropriate peek. For larger occasions such as Trooping the Colour (The Queen's Official Birthday Parade), Royal Ascot, the Royal Windsor Horse Show, and everything in-between - I have attempted to be there.

While travelling up and down the United Kingdom, often following The Queen's tours, I have noticed how she truly is in the "happiness business." Because she is an a-political figurehead, many revere her as a symbol of the nation and the Commonwealth, and not a symbol of any one political party.

The Queen in Derby, 1 April 2010 (Photograph by Andrew Lannerd).

The happiness and joy she brings is most apparent when you see The Queen interact with children. I witnessed this myself after a polo match in June 2018. Earlier that day she had been horse riding, hosted a luncheon at Windsor Castle, then travelled in a carriage procession to Royal Ascot where she watched five races and presented a trophy to the winner. Late in the afternoon she arrived at Guards Polo Club in Windsor Great Park for her annual tradition of taking tea with some of the pupils from Eton College. I observed her at certain points during the day and must admit that even I was a bit exhausted by her schedule. The Queen was 92 at the time.

After tea and the completion of a polo match the time came for her departure. There were three children lined up just outside of the royal box eager to present her with flowers, while myself with a few other people were standing just behind the children. It had been a long day, an exhausting day, and a warm one as well, but Her Majesty walked out of the royal box and over to the children. I listened as she said while showing much enthusiasm, "Oh, are those flowers for me? Thank you very much. How kind of you." It was *extraordinary* to witness. She was taking extra time to have a moment with each child.

Keep in mind, receiving bouquets is something she has done many thousands of times during her long reign. What I witnessed on this occasion was genuine kindness. It was as if no one had ever presented her with flowers before. There were no cameras in sight. After a long day the natural response would be a simple, quick, "Thank you" then moving on to relax. Instead The Queen took the time to create a huge amount of happiness for each child and ultimately for all of us present.

The Queen in Liverpool, 22 June 2016 (Photograph by Andrew Lannerd).

When you are in The Queen's presence you remember it for the rest of your life. You will, just as I am now, *cherish* the experience and tell others your story. I have seen entire villages come alive with excitement as thousands of locals gather with bunting and flags to celebrate her arrival. How many politicians would be able to bring people together like that? If they did, we know it would be short lived.

Now of course, there are individuals who think the monarchy is a relic of the past, but a majority of people living in the United Kingdom would *not* want to change the current system. Her Majesty has always enjoyed highly favourable approval ratings.

The Queen at Guards Polo Club, 18 June 2014 (Photograph by Andrew Lannerd).

How exactly does a head of state for nearly 70 years maintain this popularity? I think it lies in her unwavering devotion to duty. She has given her entire life to the service of her people, not only within the United Kingdom, but also in the 15 other countries where she is their queen. Her role as Head of the Commonwealth and duty to keep the organisation thriving is another great achievement. Today the Commonwealth is a voluntary association of 54 independent and equal countries, and home to 2.4 billion people.

The Queen's role as Head of the Commonwealth has made her the most widely travelled monarch the world has ever known, taking her to 116 countries on 266 official visits, travelling an estimated 1,032,513 miles to date.

Throughout the years during royal visits I have met some unique personalities. Odds are, if The Queen is undertaking a public engagement, along with the locals there will be a group of ten to fifteen others. The Queen has even referred to us as, "The Travellers," which is ironic considering the amount of travelling *she* has undertaken. Perhaps the reference is because it doesn't matter if it is in a small village in Scotland or the city centre of Leeds, we'll all be there if at all possible. Within this group of "fans", some are there to take photographs, while others hope for the chance of a royal interaction. We all have one thing in common - a deep interest, fascination, and respect for the monarchy. Some of us have become friends, but at the end of the day we are all after the same thing - the best possible placement for ourselves during a royal event - even if that is in front of the other's camera. Of course it is all done in good fun, but with a highly competitive edge. We have waited for countless hours in cold, heat, sun, and rain, and it is usually worth it in the end. Sometimes you are in the right spot for a royal visit, other times not, but the more of these you attend, the more you know that arriving early is key to ensure the best possible position.

I am often asked if I think The Queen recognises me. Well, she's certainly never said, "Oh, it's you again," but she doesn't forget a face, so I suspect she *might* recognise me. Her security team certainly *do* recognise me, since in the years between 2002 and 2020, I have seen Her Majesty in-person on over 250 occasions, from regional visits to public and private events.

A wonderful image circulated by the BBC, Bury St. Edmunds, 9 April 2009.

From cheering The Queen as she appears on the balcony of Buckingham Palace to standing in the pouring rain outside Westminster Abbey on the 60th wedding anniversary of The Queen and The Duke of Edinburgh, there is not much I have yet to see during these royal occasions.

Capturing Her Majesty in London, 22 May 2019.

In 2008, I travelled to Northern Ireland for the Royal Maundy service in Armagh. The enormous security operations that were put in place were astonishing. Locals in the Catholic side of town were protesting the royal visit, while people on the Protestant side were celebrating - all while tanks moved around town and low-flying helicopters patrolled overhead. To put it mildly, it was an eye-opening experience!

***

By 2010, I was making eight trips a year to the UK and back, all of which I successfully managed alongside my day-job. When not on royal pursuits I could be found in the United States working hard to support my interests.

While I enjoyed my position with the Indianapolis Symphony Orchestra, it was, after five years, becoming a little too familiar. It seemed the perfect time to make a change and pursue a new direction, but leaving the symphony was a major decision. One I did not take lightly. The patrons and my employees had become a surrogate family. We had shared so many experiences and made many memories. During the party for my departure a valued employee told me amid her tears, "You have been the best boss I have ever had." This colleague was in her 70s at the time and had held countless jobs. That was the ultimate compliment, very humbling, and one that I still cherish.

Despite the emotional hardship of leaving a job that I loved it was time to live in London and enjoy the city in ways that only a resident could do. Visiting a few times each year was great, but I needed the stability and experience of living in London, even if that was only for a short time at that stage.

My mantra was, "A life with no regrets." So I saved up my money, left my job, and came to live in London for six months in 2010. I departed the US with two suitcases in hand and a steely resolve that all would be well. I didn't know what the future held, I just knew that Britain was calling me then and there. I had to answer the call. It was an invigorating experience boarding the plane with only the future and my dreams ahead of me.

The next few months would be instrumental for the founding of a tour company that had yet to take shape, for cultivating great friendships, and for developing my interest and love for English country houses. Every day in London seemed to offer a plethora of art openings, exhibitions, and museums, as well as royal events. My spirit thrived on the variety London had to offer, as well as its countless cultural delights.

That summer I enjoyed long lunches with friends, and The Wolseley became a favourite spot. During one of these meals we sat next to the eccentric, yet renowned painter, Lucian Freud, who famously threw his bread rolls across the restaurant at a group of Americans that were relentlessly taking his picture. When the Americans complained to management the response was, "I'm sorry but Mr. Freud can do what he likes at The Wolseley."

Just as Lucian Freud was to The Wolseley so was Raine, Countess Spencer (stepmother to Diana, Princess of Wales) to The Ritz. I once had a brief conversation with her in The Rivoli Bar, her hair coiffed to the ceiling in its usual iconic manner. She complained of the heavy traffic due to people returning from Royal Ascot. I smiled and found that ironic since she had a full-time chauffeur who had just dropped her off.

Later that summer an event was held in the gardens of Clarence House, the London residence of The Prince of Wales. The celebration was to acknowledge and promote environmental sustainability. I booked two timed tickets, knowing that Charles and his wife Camilla, The Duchess of Cornwall, would be attending on that specific morning. I invited Elaine Klemesrud to join me as she was visiting London that week. Elaine had been a colleague at the Indiana State Museum, and she had become a cherished friend.

Before the royal arrival, we both noticed a marquee encouraging guests to make a reusable carrier bag out of old fabric. The printed sign in front read, "The Prince of Wales has kindly donated curtain material from Clarence House. Enter-to-win this fabric." I immediately marched inside and said, "I'd like to enter to win the royal fabric, please." To which I received a rather stuffy reply, "Well, of course, but we have yet to find the winner, and so many have tried."

One could enter-to-win by sticking their hand into a large basket. Only by pulling out a special coloured ball would the royal drapery be won. In went my hand and, to my great delight, I pulled out the winning ball! "Wonderful!" I said letting out a little laugh. The astonished look on the face of the stuffy attendant was priceless.

Fantastic! I had now won a section of the beautiful old curtains donated by The Prince of Wales - great, fabulous. I wanted to take them and leave, but was quickly informed by the same pompous attendant, "Oh no. You have to make a carrier bag out of them!" I responded, "Oh really, I can't just take the fabric?" "No," came the supercilious reply, "and you'll find the sewing machine over there."

It truly was a sight! I had never touched a sewing machine before, and yet, there I was, sitting in the gardens of Clarence House sewing a bag out of Prince Charles' old curtains. How ridiculous, yet that carrier bag and the story that goes along with it still makes me smile.

Not long after the sewing incident we re-joined the event. By then The Prince of Wales and The Duchess of Cornwall were mingling with guests. To our great amusement, a musician started to give a short "royal command performance" on a very usual instrument - a keyboard cleverly disguised so it looked as if it was made of stuffed cats.

His performance of *Somewhere Over the Rainbow* was done with the sounds of meowing cats. There was a loud "meow" with each key he played. It was beyond hilarious, and no one present (including the royal couple) could keep a straight face. The newspaper reports the next day said it all - "Prince Charles and Camilla in fits of laughter at crazy cat piano."

With the Prince of Wales just after the "sewing incident," 12 September 2010.

During those months of living in London I travelled at every opportunity to see the great country houses of Britain. This time spent exploring the great estates of the country would lay the groundwork for my future business - but that was still down the line.

I returned to the United States that autumn, my mind filled with memories and determination that at some point I would live permanently in the United Kingdom. In the meantime, the need to be fiscally responsible kicked in. It was time to return to the comfort of a consistent, salaried position.

Luckily for me, my next position would be one that I would greatly enjoy. I became the General Manager for the Indianapolis Symphonic Choir. It was such a pleasure to support and assist the mission and growth of the organisation. At the start of my tenure the choir was producing concerts in local churches, in addition to their performances alongside the Indianapolis Symphony Orchestra. This was inexpensive but *not* at the level I felt the artistic excellence merited. When we were forced to balance seating our guests while a baptism was taking place in the lobby, I quickly made it clear that it was time we stepped up our game and perform in actual concert venues. No more churches. We made the change and the next year we began to sell out large professional theatres. Previously only a few hundred guests attended our "church performances."

I enjoyed my time with the choir a great deal; planning fundraising galas, and of course, performances. In addition to managing some of the day-to-day operations, two highlights stand out from my experiences as General Manager. The first was planning and executing a concert tour, taking 250 people to Carnegie Hall in New York City. The other was orchestrating a significant concert tour to The Kennedy Center in Washington, D.C. Both tours involved chartering flights, taking over large hotels, and planning receptions and events, as well as concert logistics and promotions. Designing and implementing tours on such a large scale was so satisfying.

One day I was asked by colleagues how I would feel about putting together a new donor opportunity for our patrons. It was to be a group tour of England focusing on the music of composer Benjamin Britten. Since my knowledge of the UK was already established, the organisation felt that I was best suited to plan, manage, and facilitate the tour.

It took a year of planning, and I found great pleasure - delight really - in making sure every detail was covered. Building a budget, selecting hotels, sights, restaurants, and working with vendors to deliver a unique experience for the tour guests.

The week was a huge success. At the tour's final dinner in London, I felt emotional as our guests told me how much they had enjoyed their experience. It felt like a testimonial and made me proud of my many hours of planning. At the end of the evening everyone was asking, "Where are we going next year Andrew?"

I had found something special. Perhaps the young boy in search for the wider world with his travel brochures had finally made his mark?

I knew there had to be other tours.

I had discovered joy in sharing my passion with others. They wanted more. I wanted more. I knew I had to find a way to make it happen.

Chapter Four:
The Makings of a Company

Transcendent Surpassing the ordinary; exceptional

That had to be the name of the company. Yes, Transcendent Travel.

After locking myself in a room to brainstorm for an entire day, I knew that had to be the name. In actuality, the process for choosing the company name can be traced back to a single conversation in Chicago.

I had already known Kathryn Rice for a few years. She was a successful executive, as well as a board member for the Indianapolis Symphonic Choir, my full-time employer at the time. Kathryn had become a friend, and was a tour participant on the first group tour that I had taken to England, a tour focusing on the music of Benjamin Britten.

She lived in Chicago and frequently I spent weekends there, as my schedule allowed. One afternoon as we were walking along Lake Michigan and I mentioned how much I had enjoyed planning the Benjamin Britten tour. I shared how, in planning that tour I felt that I had found my calling. Since she'd been one of my tour guests she could see the potential and said, "Well, why don't we start a business?"

Kathryn had been successful for many years working for large American firms such as Deloitte, as was well known for getting things done. So when she made the suggestion it certainly carried some weight. I quickly replied, "OK. Yes, let's do it," not really knowing what starting a business from the ground up would entail.

In her usual way, she ran with it, and the next thing I knew she was busily putting in place the legal paperwork required to get us started. We talked more and more about what the company could look like, and how we could set ourselves apart from others in the industry. What would we call the company?

For years, I had dreamed about the types of experiences I wanted to cultivate. Our tours had to be unique and special. I was not interested in merely taking groups to places that anyone could do on their own. My desire, and ultimately our intensions have always been to offer tours that provide opportunities and access to unusual locations.

When I locked myself in the room to come up with a name for our business, I knew that the company needed to reflect tour experiences that were rare, memorable, and treasured by our tour participants. *Transcendent Travel* eventually came to mind. The burning question was, did another organisation already have the name? It was such a good name, so I began researching. We were pleased to learn that it was not being used by an active company, so shortly after the company was formed, and as soon as was legally permissible the trademark application was filed in the United States and in the United Kingdom. Both of which were eventually granted.

Co-founders of companies must each bring different talents to the table, and that is certainly true for us. Kathryn has vast experience in business operations (back of house), while I lean towards the creative side and the packaging of our product (front of house). Together our diverse strengths were the assets we needed to build and grow the company.

During the first few years as we developed our business, we conducted one or two group tours a year. This was fine at the time since we were slowly building a client base and our reputation. During that time I was also polishing my skills as a tour director.

Two tours were not enough to earn a sustainable income, so I was working full-time while building the business on the side. This involved working countless late nights, often spent in coffee shops. In Indianapolis I would leave my office at the end of the day, head home, change and collect my laptop, then head to a coffee shop to work on tours. Frequently I would work until around 10:00 pm, so I preferred spots that served a light-bite, so I could have dinner while I worked.

In order to stay on target during this busy period I was known to schedule time allotments with friends. Personal relationships at this stage were also "kept at arm's length." There just wasn't any extra time. This continued for a couple of years. Hard yes, but necessary in order to achieve my goals.

It was a huge amount of work, and eventually the time came for me to commit myself fully to Transcendent Travel. I was convinced we could make it work and I was keen to put everything into making it happen. I was confident that the time and effort we invested would pay off in the end.

Anyone that has started a business will know the challenges involved. Setting up a legal entity, building a brand, creating a website, building social media and a client base, delivering the product, and paying taxes - all need attention to detail without losing sight of the big picture. Building a company with a presence in two countries also proved challenging, but we got there in the end.

While the work was relentless at times, in many ways I found it to be invigorating. When I wasn't on the road I'd be planning to be on the road, and best of all, I was curating experiences for people. Experiences that, hopefully, they would enjoy and never forget. Managing it all was a challenge, but the end result was so rewarding.

In the early days we attempted to offer experiences in New York City and Chicago, as well as in the UK. These offerings, while unique, failed to gain traction so we decided to focus more on our niche opportunities in the United Kingdom.

Most entrepreneurs who surpass the breaking point can recall the moment that changed the game for them. For us it involved creating partnerships with Public Broadcasting Service (PBS) stations, an American public broadcaster and television program distributor. Then Acorn TV, an online television streaming service, became a partner. Both PBS and Acorn TV collaborated with us to curate unique British television tours in the UK.

Quality British television shows have always been my passion. When I was young I often watched the BBC adaptation of *Pride and Prejudice*, as well as *Keeping Up Appearances*, which is still a favourite of mine. The hilarious antics of Hyacinth Bucket (pronounced *Bouquet*) never fails to amuse me for her social climbing, which is often disrupted by her dysfunctional family. To me it seemed obvious that anyone passionate about these types of shows would also be interested in going to see the sights associated with them in England. The series *Downton Abbey®* was just becoming popular at the time in the United States, and why would viewers *not* want to see Highclere Castle for themselves? But why just Highclere? Why not create an entire seven-day experience surrounding British television?

I started brainstorming, put together my ideas, and presented the tour concept to WFYI, the Indianapolis, Indiana-based PBS affiliate. My proposal was met with some interest, but it would still be some time before I got them to sign on. I had planted the seed and had to wait. It took time and others in the community to water it.

A few months after the initial meeting I was having a conversation with a lady who had been on one of my tours. She said, "Oh, I just saw the team at WFYI, and I was telling them how good your tours are." She was influential in the community, so I hoped her message would quickly filter through to decision-makers at the station. I learned that others had also mentioned my tour. Then it happened - WFYI approached me and said, "We'd love to partner on a tour."

What a moment that was! I was elated.

Richard Miles was at WFYI at the time, and together we enjoyed discussing the first tour. While I designed the tour, he would occasionally suggest, "What about this programme?" Then I would think about logistics and research tour options surrounding it. We were creating something special for their viewers. That experience was so rewarding.

Once we successfully designed and executed tours in this niche market, we were able to attract Acorn TV to our developing portfolio. Other member-station PBS markets also signed on. It was a game changer, and eventually it became apparent that it was time to leave my full-time job and go all in with Transcendent Travel.

I remember the excitement the first time I saw a TV spot for one of my tours. It was on a Sunday evening right before an episode of *Downton Abbey*. That was a proud moment. My hard work and passion were beginning to pay off.

Our first hire was Elaine Klemesrud, who I introduced you to earlier. Having worked with her at the Indiana State Museum I knew she was a natural choice for the Transcendent Travel team. Her passion for customer service, love of travel, and professionalism is appreciated by not only our clients, but also by Kathryn and me.

I am especially proud of our partnership with Acorn TV and our yearly "Best of Acorn TV Tours." Growing up, I recall my excitement when the Acorn catalogue arrived in the mail. I carefully read each page, and when finished it would join my vast collection of pamphlets. Any Anglophile may remember the Acorn catalogues filled with British telly videos and interesting British products. I sometimes wish that I could whisper to that teenager pouring over each page of the catalogue, "One day, you'll be leading tours for Acorn TV." To be trusted as the only tour company to offer UK tours for Acorn TV subscribers is an honour and a privilege, and that is not lost on me.

Transcendent Travel tours have been mentioned in *The New York Times as* well as in *Architectural Digest*. The biggest honour for me was my January 2019 interview and one-page spread in *The Times*, London. The article was about the niche we carved out for ourselves in the British tourism market.

I am often asked if things ever go wrong on tours. Of course! There have been many memorable, hilarious, and challenging situations that have occurred while on the road. Things can happen when hosting 30 people for a week. Could it be the guest that arrived with empty suitcases (they had forgotten to pack their belongings)? Or perhaps being asked if it is safe to drink the water in England? Not everyone arrives on tour with the same level of travel experience, and I enjoy that very much. There isn't much I have yet to see or hear while on tour. It all adds to the fun and creates variety, which can be welcome when I am running the same tour for multiple weeks back-to-back.

It was the final dinner of the tour and the week had gone very well. I was hosting a farewell meal in central London, when out of the corner of my eye, I observed as a large mouse ran from an open window INTO the dining room where my guests were enjoying their main course. I knew that I must act…carefully.

I didn't want to alarm anyone, yet I could just envision this mouse turning a civilised dinner into total chaos. While continuing to engage in the conversation, I cautiously kept one eye on the mouse, *praying* that no one else would notice. Though composed I was definitely distracted. Then just as quickly as he came, the mouse headed towards the windowsill. Without hesitation I excused myself from the table, bolted towards it, and as graciously as I could, brushed him out of the window - shutting it quickly. Mr. Mouse was now outside looking in, as I breathed a sigh of relief. The dinner continued - crisis averted.

The tours I curate tend to attract kind and interesting people, many well-travelled, all of whom share a commonality in the core theme of any given tour. Quite a few tour guests come back and take a different tour each year, and it is great to see so many familiar faces. Even after positive feedback from tour participants there is always room for improvement, and that is what I am consistently striving to do. It may be adjusting dinner menus or perhaps agenda timings based on feedback that I receive.

It is so satisfying to observe as guests who arrive as strangers, meet on tour, and become friends. Even more satisfying is when these new friends return to take tours together. Sometimes tour participants become my personal friends. Which for me is an unexpected bonus. Though it is rewarding to watch how friendships grow as the tour unfolds, there are times when things don't go so well. I have had the unfortunate experience to observe close friends who've never travelled together discover they were not as compatible as they once thought! These moments add to the adventure of another week on the road, and no two group dynamics are the same.

Watching tour guests enjoying themselves is the best part of all.

One group may have a few comedians along, which always livens things up, while another group is more serious, and yet another is more introverted. The introverted crowd is often the toughest since I have no idea what they are thinking until the last days of the tour. It is my job to make sure that, no matter the demographics of the group, everyone has a great time.

You might be surprised to discover that it takes about a year to research and design a new tour for our portfolio. This involves a great deal of careful planning and consideration regarding drive times and accommodation options. I also look carefully at what attractions are available, and love identifying the unique ingredients which make our tours different and sought after. It is important that a week's itinerary has something for everyone. So, I pay careful attention to the diversity of the itinerary when planning.

Once I feel comfortable with a new tour concept, I am off to that area for a few days of meetings, research, and planning. This involves, among other things, meeting with hotel staff, choosing restaurants, timing myself on walks (always walking slower than I normally would to replicate navigating a large group), and meeting local tour guides and hiring them to give me a tour. I enjoy these site visits very much, and love planning the many details and experiences that make a tour special.

Sampling local delicacies is a treat. When planning a tour on the Isle of Wight, I selected a waterside hotel in large part because their restaurant is renowned for fresh mussels. The group I ended up bringing on the tour were mostly from middle America, nowhere near the sea, and getting them to sample this superb local dish proved a little harder than I had foreseen.

At the beginning of dinner I could tell they were not impressed that I had pre-selected mussels for their entrée. Most stared at the bowls for a moment, while one guest dared to dive in. His subsequent exclamation and appetite inspired the others to join in. From the looks on their faces, I knew I had delivered an unforgettable meal.

I have the same experience when I take groups to Cornwall, which is renowned for exceptional seafood. Any guests that have taken part in my Port Isaac dinners know that I select the courses that everyone will eat unless there are special requests or allergies. Port Isaac is a Cornish fishing village, so the chef prepares a delicious white seabass served with a beautiful salad and new potatoes. When the plates are presented I might get a look, but once they sample it they begin to rave.

In my opinion the job of a good tour director is highlighting what makes a region exceptional. Some people would simply choose to order chicken, but when you expand your palate, you discover that instead of a plain piece of chicken, you could have fresh fish that was caught along the coast that very morning. Managing guest expectations while encouraging people to try new things is a fine line, but I find my guests are usually up to the challenge.

With tour guests in Scotland, September 2019.

Then there are the hotels - these can be tricky at times. A good sales director will attempt to show me only their very best rooms, so I often surprise them with my desire to see their lowest category of room. If one wing has been renovated I ask to see the unrenovated wing. I do this so that I know if there are any rooms to avoid when planning rooming allocations with the staff. During these visits I see quite a few bedrooms, and with a rather mischievous grin I have been known to say, "I have seen more hotel rooms in this country than almost anyone else."

As an American producing tours in the United Kingdom for North American guests, I have a unique insight and understanding that a British tour director wouldn't have. For example, because I am American, I understand the expectations and nuisances of Americans when they travel. In the United States when you have a three-course meal served to a large group, the guests generally expect the plates to be cleared as soon as over half of the people eating have completed their course.

Tour guests having a little fun in Cornwall.

Well, that would be considered rude in Britain. Traditionally in Britain, *no* plates are to be removed until *every* person at the table has *finished*. If a certain guest is a slow eater and chatting, then a North American audience might start to think that the service was lagging if empty plates linger. When in actually the next course is waiting in the kitchen.

My job is a delicate dance between my knowledge about North American guests and the traditions in Britain. Here is another example - Americans like to drink coffee *with* their dessert. In Britain coffee, like tea is a separate event *after* dessert. I work closely with the hospitality teams to manage guest expectations while also respecting their service arrangements. There's never a dull moment when on the road.

Along the way I have parted ways with hotels and vendors. I enjoy working with hotels over multiple years, but becoming too familiar with the staff can have the unintended consequence of diminished service. In a travel business where service is our differentiator, that's simply unacceptable. When "becoming too familiar" happens, errors pop up. I must be alert and intervene before these changes become evident to our tour guests.

I delight in delivering surprises. The "big reveal" is my favourite moment during any given tour. Whether that's surprising the group with a celebrity visit during dinner, or having a bagpipe player greet guests in Scotland as they walk up a red carpet to board the *Royal Yacht Britannia,* the looks of delight by my unexpected guests are the snapshots that line my memory. Along the way I've delighted in surprising guests with actors, authors, and on occasion an unannounced historian or curator.

A luncheon at Highclere Castle, June 2018.

My guests were unsuspecting as they boarded the coach to find a sealed envelope on each of their seats. I kindly asked everyone to wait to open their envelope until all were present and relished in the thought of what was coming. As they simultaneously opened their envelope, the heading on their card featured The Prince of Wales feathers and read, "You're invited to a champagne afternoon tea and tour of the private gardens of The Prince of Wales at Highgrove."

They had been promised "gardens in the Cotswolds" that morning, and that is exactly what they got. On the coach the elation was palpable and then came a round of applause. I had known this would happen for months but wanted it to remain a surprise for the very reason I had just witnessed - the joy and excitement on their faces.

When recalling the many unforgettable tour moments, above all, there is one ultimate stand out experience. In May 2019, I had the opportunity to host a very special tour that took guests behind-the-scenes in Windsor. We called it, "Windsor & The Great Park: A Royal Heritage Weekend." When I was approached with the opportunity it came with one unbreakable clause - *discretion*.

The guests stayed in a former royal residence and were treated to special access to areas that were normally off limits to the general public. They were prepared in advance with protocols, and background checks were required. The highlight of the weekend was the chance for tour guests to attend Sunday morning services in the private chapel in Windsor Great Park. This exclusive opportunity was a privilege, but it could not be advertised as a selling point for the tour. The brochure simply mentioned that guests would attend services there, but in no way could refer to the chance that "someone special" might also be in attendance.

Members of the royal family have worshiped in this small, intimate chapel since the reign of Queen Victoria. It is positioned in Windsor Great Park next to Royal Lodge. Since I had previously attended services in the chapel I knew what to expect. Regardless, my mind was racing with thoughts of "will she or won't she be here" the entire time.

The service was about to start, and my tour guests and I were all seated in the chapel. We heard a car pulling up outside, then watched as a suited protection officer took his position in the front of the chapel. Her Majesty The Queen had indeed arrived, and the service started with the congregation standing to sing the National Anthem.

You can imagine their excitement. My tour guests were attending a Sunday service with (cue the fanfare), *"Elizabeth the Second, by the Grace of God, of the United Kingdom of Great Britain and Northern Ireland and of Her other Realms and Territories Queen, Head of the Commonwealth, Defender of the Faith"* in *her* private chapel.

At the end of the service my guests lined up near The Queen's car. From the side I watched with great pride as each of them in turn gave her the appropriate bow or curtsy as she emerged from the chapel. Standing back I felt like a proud parent and beamed, smiling at their impeccable timing. Until now no one had seen The Queen since the royal box is hidden from the congregational view during the service. Then she emerged in soft pink wearing a gorgeous diamond brooch that sparkled in sun. The Queen approached my guests and said, "Don't you all look lovely today." Then continued, "Are you staying at Cumberland Lodge?" "Yes," was their reply as she bestowed her warm and gracious smile on us.

As The Queen departed I turned to look at one of my guests. Her eyes were filled with tears, revealing the emotion brought on by what she had just experienced. We had all been graced with the presence of the head of state, a monarch, and an icon that had gone out of her way to show us kindness - likely understanding that the moment would remain with us always.

At the end of 2019, another one of my guests that had participated in the tour wrote to me to say that attending the service and interacting with The Queen was the highlight of their year. Moments like these encapsulate why I love what I do. Sharing the places I love in a carefully curated way allows me the opportunity to create memories that will last a lifetime - for myself, and more importantly, for my tour guests.

Often as I go about the work, I am reminded of the quote, "Choose a job you love, and you will never have to work a day in your life."

Indeed. I am fortunate in that regard.

Chapter Five: Collecting

The Wallace Collection and the Victoria & Albert Museum (The V&A) in London are two places that I love to roam at every available opportunity. What could be better than a Sunday morning exploring the many corridors and galleries filled with exquisite decorative arts, often acquired and later donated by generations of great collectors. Years ago at The Wallace Collection I came across a quotation that frequently comes to the forefront of my mind, "My collection is the result of my life."

Every passionate collector will appreciate the joy of finding unique objects, sometimes when you least expect it. Then comes the pleasure of looking after it, and most thrilling of all - sharing your treasures with others.

Surrounded by a few of my treasures.

For me it has never been enough to simply read about and visit the sites associated with history. I have always had a strong desire to own objects directly associated with my interests and travels. I've concluded that collector typifies me in so many ways.

Not only do I collect objects, but I collect memories. Throughout history, psychologists have studied the varied reasons why people collect. According to Wikipedia:

"For people who collect, the value of their collections is not monetary but emotional. The collections allow people to relive their childhood, connect themselves to a period or to a time they feel strongly about. Their collections help them ease insecurity and anxiety about losing a part of themselves and to keep the past to continue to exist in the present. Some collect for the thrill of the hunt. For these collectors, collecting is a quest, a lifelong pursuit which can never be completed."

Sigmund Freud famously focused on a more "dark side" motivation in his studies of the psychology of collecting. When I read these studies, I acknowledge some traits, but not all, in myself.

No two collectors are the same. I know of people that hide away their collections, only sharing them with selected individuals when trust has been established. Other collectors place their prized treasures in a vault, only peeking at the objects on rare occasions. Others are in fact hoarders who fill their homes with every possible item, often never parting with anything, while some are easily swayed and sell their collectable shortly after purchasing it to move onto the next item.

The factors in why individuals collect are varied and complicated. At the surface level I see myself as preserving history. Being surrounded by beautiful objects reminds me of the places or periods of history that I love. These objects may also represent times of joy or life experiences.

As far as I am concerned, if there's a surface, it should be covered in objects!

To rescue a wonderful object from an unappreciative owner or to have something restored to its original glory is also most rewarding. As people walk into my home I want them to feel transported into a unique space that has been lovingly curated. When guests arrive I always like to say something outrageous such as, "I'm such a minimalist," or, "I am sorry there is nothing to see here," - which usually gets a laugh.

Visitors quickly notice that I am not an album collector. I don't conceal everything neatly away in books, instead I love having my collection on full display for people to enjoy. If I need to hide the object away I am not particularly interested in owning it.

In addition to rescuing, restoring, and displaying, the stories of how I may have stumbled onto a particular piece can be such fun.

From antique markets to eBay®, from auction houses to flea markets, I've accumulated many stories about going the extra mile to obtain something new for my collection. One of my favourite stories happened in 2013 in Stratford-upon-Avon when, as usual, I was exploring the area for antiques.

When entering antique shops, I often ask, "Do you have any unusual royal items?" That usually drives home the point that I am not looking for a teacup with The Queen's face on it. Those are a dime a dozen. That day my inquiry was met with, "No, I don't think so." I thanked him and walked out of the shop.

Nearly into the next block and about to turn the corner, I heard the man yelling, "Come back! Come back!" I returned to the shop where he revealed, "I think I might have something of interest to you. That is if I can find it." Diving into a small chaotic room he emerged a few moments later, pulling a large swath of fabric out of a dilapidated cardboard tube. Unrolling it onto the table in front of me, inside… just inside… I gasped.

It was a large piece of the original silk that had hung in Westminster Abbey during The Queen's coronation on 2 June 1953. The silk pattern is called "Queensway", and it is very difficult to find. It depicts St. Edward's Crown and shows the flowers of the realm - the rose of England, the thistle for Scotland, the shamrock for Northern Ireland, and the leek that represents Wales. It was woven in Essex, and was luxurious at the time since Britain was just emerging from post-war austerity.

I knew exactly what was in front of me. Inside I was screaming and jumping up and down, but outside I was playing it cool as a cucumber, acting as if I might be *vaguely* interested. I had tried to acquire another piece of this fabric earlier that year, but it far surpassed auction estimates and sold for a couple of thousand pounds.

The shopkeeper mentioned that he'd owned the fabric for well over 30 years but had forgotten about it. He continued, "You know it's been sitting here for a while, so I'd be happy to take £100 for it." I don't think I've ever paid for anything so quickly. I knew I had to leave before he changed his mind or came to the realisation that he was basically giving it away. Grinning like the Cheshire Cat I slipped out of the shop.

Stories like this only encourage a collector to keep searching. It becomes a game of being more knowledgeable than the person selling the object and reacting quickly in a shrewd manner.

In London there are Sunday morning ephemera fairs which turn up gems from time-to-time. Before the start of the fair there is always a queue outside filled with eager collectors. Those of us waiting might catch up with a friend in the queue, but then it is "game on" and competitive excitement as the doors open. The tables in the room are filled with numerous books, documents and ephemera all waiting to be discovered.

On a nondescript Sunday a few years ago the fair doors opened and I started my usual speedy, yet focused perusal. In a way you feel like a pig snorting out truffles, for within the piles of paper are gems waiting to be discovered. Then you see them, stop and think to yourself, "could it be?" No? Is it? Oh my…

What did I see that day, perched on a dealer's table off in the distance? Two coronets.

In the paper fair filled with documents they were an anachronism. I hurried over to the table and picked them up, one large and one small. Made of deep red velvet and ermine, with gold bases and intricate gold braid tops, they looked completely right to me. Still, I wanted another opinion just in case. I asked the price and the dealer said, "£300 for both," which was a bargain beyond belief.

This was not the time to barter so I handed the dealer a £50 note to hold them for me, then asked him to place them under his table out of view of other potential buyers.

I then hurried off to get a second opinion from my friend Ian Shapiro. Ian is a highly regarded London specialist in stamps, autographs, and documents of royal importance. Together we returned to the dealer, studied the coronets, and Ian immediately said what I thought to be the case. "These are completely right." Once I had his reassurance, I ran to the cash machine and promptly paid for both coronets. The seller placed them in a Sainsbury's bright orange plastic grocery bag. Feeling like the cat that got the cream, I pulled out the coronets to show my fellow collector friends over coffee. And yes, we all tried on the gilded coronets as we sat and laughed in the café. Only in London.

Later that week the research commenced and I discovered that one coronet was worn by a viscount and the other by a baroness. They are solid silver gilt, and were made for the coronation of King Edward VII in 1902 by Garrard, the crown jeweller at the time. It is likely they were worn at every coronation during the 20th century (1902, 1911, 1937, and 1953). Even now, seeing my £300 coronets makes me smile, and I still wonder to this day if the dealer thought they were theatrical props rather than the real thing.

While I trusted my instinct on the coronets, it was still vital for me to have Ian's second opinion. Through the years he's become a close friend and a source of advice and inspiration. He is my collecting kindred spirit, and our friendship greatly enriches my life.

I met Ian in 2008 when I was actively collecting royal objects. At that time they tended to be items that were easier to obtain. During our first meeting in London, Ian dazzled me with letters written by The Queen, signed royal images, and presentation gifts - often bearing engraved royal cyphers.

Once it became apparent that with a little money and knowledge I too could own these types of objects, my collecting taste matured.

I can point to many objects in my collection that are a direct result of being friends with Ian, and we are still frequently found talking about a new object, going to a fair together, or discussing the latest auction.

Years ago, Ian and I travelled to Brighton to pick up two 1953 coronation chairs that we had purchased. One chair would be for him, the other for me. For coronations that took place in the 20th century, the chairs used by the guests in Westminster Abbey, could be purchased after the event by the individual. That is why so many of the great country houses in England have coronation chairs in their drawing rooms.

We enjoyed a warm day in Brighton, but once we collected the chairs it was time to cart them back to London. Imagine the sight as both of us carried our chair, walking all the way through Brighton and uphill to the train station. When we finally got on the train, we were pleased to find a large space where we could place the chairs and sit across from them. As the train left the station we began to relax and started to talk. The next thing we knew, a very large man attempted to sit on one of our chairs. Perhaps he didn't know, or wasn't bothered that it was *not* a normal seat. Luckily Ian noticed and instantly exclaimed, "No, no, no! You CANNOT sit there." Startled, the enormous man got the idea and quickly moved on as we started to laugh at what had just transpired.

Later that same chair went bubble wrapped into the cargo hold of an airplane. Upon arrival, with the chair at Chicago O'Hare, I was pulled aside and watched it being scanned for bugs by US Homeland Security. They asked me what kind of chair it was. I replied, "A coronation chair." Seeing their faces they had *no* idea what on *earth* that was, so they quickly moved me along.

Once the chair made it safely to my collection, it joined 600 books on the royal family, signed presentation photographs, letters, and ephemera, as well as boxed pieces of royal wedding cakes, and china and glassware used for entertaining in the royal palaces.

A few interesting objects in my collection include additional coronation chairs, a pair of suede gloves worn by Wallis Simpson, The Duchess of Windsor, A portrait of King George VI by Sir Gerald Kelly, painted during the Second World War at Windsor Castle, as well as childhood drawings and notes written by Princess Elizabeth, later to become Queen Elizabeth II.

People often ask me how I acquire my objects. It could be at an auction, or online, or from another collector. But above all, for me, it is all about the provenance. Often personal gifts and letters are purchased after the passing of the recipient. Like all heirs who inherit items of value not everything is kept, and that is a major source for some of the best material.

Whether travelling great distances to pick up an object, carrying enormous paintings thru train stations, or flying across the Atlantic with a large marble bust on my lap, there isn't much I haven't done in the pursuit of my collection. When I was living in the United States, my alarm would frequently go off in the early morning hours in order to bid over the telephone at an auction.

I consider myself a caretaker of what are, in many cases, small pieces of the past that will live on as records of history long after my life comes to an end. I spend large amounts of time caring for my collection as well. From dusting and polishing to restoration and insurance policies, there is much work involved with maintaining a collection.

Through the years I have acquired objects that for various reasons were not previously cared for, and it is a joy to have things restored to their former glory. From crumbling frames to dirty canvases, every collector who invests energy in restoration knows the joy that comes from revitalising what would otherwise have been lost.

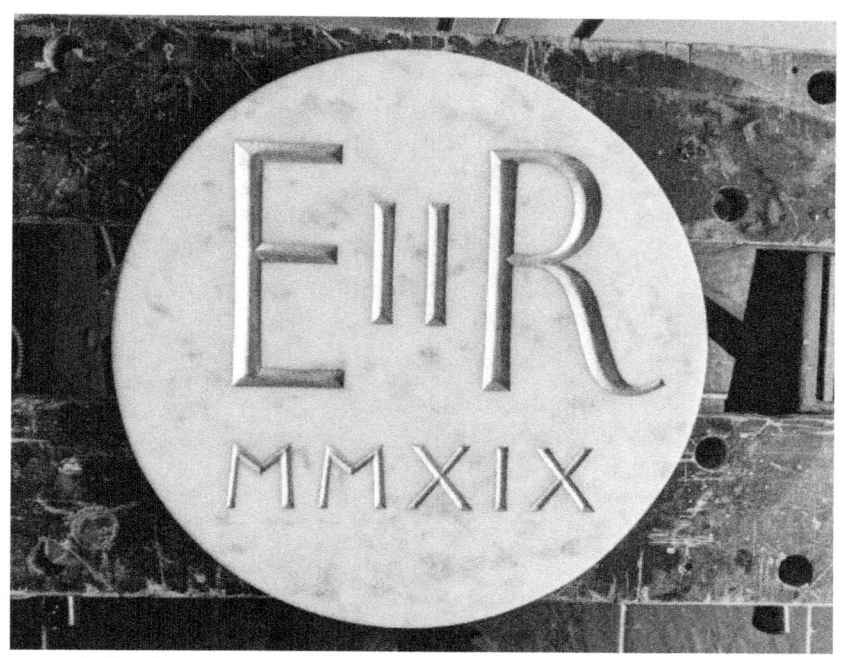

A commission from Wayne Hart in 2019. The Queen's cypher, hand carved and gilded in Carrara Marble.

I also greatly enjoy the process of commissioning new works of art and collaborating directly with artists to produce something special.

Nothing was more rewarding than working with my close friend, Rosanna Hardin Hall, on a painting to celebrate The Queen becoming the longest serving British monarch in 2015.

Rosanna, a respected artist from Indianapolis, had been a friend for a few years and I was always impressed by her great skills as a painter. We worked closely together on the painting for a year. This involved initial sketches, thinking about and planning symbolism, talking through colours, and finally getting the painting *just* right. We unveiled the finished work at an event in her Indianapolis gallery on the day that The Queen's reign surpassed that of Queen Victoria in September 2015.

What intrigues me is how Rosanna grinds pigments and mixes her paints in a time-consuming way, all by hand. Nothing comes from a tube. This technique was mastered by artists during the Renaissance period and Rosanna was trained in this tradition when at art school in Florence, Italy.

How wonderful it is to work alongside an artist and witness the expertise and skills involved in the creation of art. For The Queen's Diamond Jubilee in 2012, I commissioned a stained-glass window, and in 2017, I commissioned a sapphire pin for the Queen's Sapphire Jubilee. And I am already looking ahead to 2022 which will likely be celebrations for a Platinum Jubilee. I had better start saving for that one!

Many pieces of my collection are a celebration of fine craftsmanship. From the beauty of post-war British silver, to the delicate hand-painting on an English enamel box, the skills involved in creating these works of art are inspiring. Owning beautiful objects enriches my life.

At home in Windsor.

Collecting for me is a daily pursuit. While I am constantly scouring the internet for the next auction, sometimes I stumble across an object when I least expect it. When in London I love exploring the antique markets, many of which are teaming with tourists and priced accordingly. Others are less well known and are a more likely source of bargains. One favourite of mine is Jubilee Market at Covent Garden on a Monday morning. I love it because the dealers there want to sell everything on their tables so they don't have to cart the items back and forth every week. Because of this you can barter and deal with the sellers there - which makes for the most fun. One *great* buy was a rather nice painting of Queen Elizabeth The Queen Mother for the "hefty" price of £15!

London's most famous street market is on Portobello Road, near Notting Hill. Saturday morning is well known for its antique market - which has attracted large crowds for many years. Sadly, I have watched the market getting noticeably smaller as antique dealers are pushed out by high rents and incoming cafés. Despite all of this, I still appreciate an occasional early morning rummage around Portobello. My rules and strategy while at the market are straight forward and based on years of experience. In the market by 7:30 am, coffee at 8:00 am, and out of the market by 9:00 am, to avoid the arrival of the tourists. Nine times out of ten I don't find anything to buy, but my nostalgia over a 2008 find keeps me coming back.

One Saturday morning in October 2008, I was looking around the market and stumbled across a beautiful oil painting with the familiar faces of two small girls. The painting was finely framed and very well-done. I played it cool, as I had recognised the faces to be those of Princesses Elizabeth and Margaret when they were children. In the painting they are playing on the beach, likely near the Sandringham Estate in Norfolk. The painting is a beautiful thing to behold. I carefully moved in to take a closer look and after a few moments, asked the dealer for the price.

To my astonishment, he did not realise the identity of the girls. Perhaps all he could see were children playing on the beach. Obviously not the two royal girls that I saw. It was to be my lucky day. We settled on a price that still makes me smile. Today it still takes pride of place in my home, and the story only adds to my enjoyment of the painting.

Sometimes there are bargains, and other times you acknowledge and react when higher prices must be paid. Eventually you learn when, and how quickly you need to "up your game" and pay more - for if you don't, someone else will.

The personalities of other collectors in my genre are varied. Some have become close friends, but there is a very real sense of competition since we may be after the same objects. At times we say to one another, "Are you bidding on anything today?" That tells the other person that you have found something without telling them exactly what you will be bidding on. You hope the answer you receive will be, "No." If it is a, "Yes," it might be time to "up your bid."

These relationships also allow the collector to "trade up" for better objects without contributing as much money as someone outside the collector's circle might need to do. My favourite story about "trading up" involves selling something that I bought in a London market for £28 and trading it for a platinum and diamond piece of royal presentation jewellery. Both sides of the deal were happy, and "trading up" allowed me to acquire something very special.

From book fairs to auction houses, and from flea markets to "trading up" opportunities, the world of collecting is a vital part of my life. So yes, I am an *unashamed* collector. And I have had such fun along the way. Perhaps I've had little *too* much fun, or *may* have gone a little over budget once or twice, but hey - you only live once!

The words of William Morris, the renowned British textile designer and poet, certainly ring true for me. "Have nothing in your home that you do not know to be useful or believe to be beautiful."

Chapter Six:
A Tale of Two Weddings

The contrast was striking. From camping out and sleeping on the ground to being an invited guest, that's how I differentiate between the weddings of Prince William in 2011 and that of his younger brother Prince Harry in 2018. So much changed for me in the span of seven years.

For centuries royal weddings were private occasions, often taking place behind closed palace doors. Beginning in the 1920s the royal family realised that these events could become national and international celebrations. The weddings evolved from small ceremonies taking place in the private chapels of royal palaces into large events of state staged in elaborate settings such as Westminster Abbey.

Royal weddings showcase the nation and the British Monarchy on an international stage and are ideal for promoting British tourism, as I have well-discovered. Before 2018, my tour guests arriving to Windsor rarely asked about St. George's Chapel. As soon as Prince Harry's wedding took place everyone started to inquire, "Will I get to see St. George's Chapel?"

Royal weddings have long had a powerful influence on the traditions of society. One profound change in custom involved the colour of the wedding dress. The white wedding dress was widely popularised by Queen Victoria when she married Prince Albert of Saxe-Coburg and Gotha in 1840.

The wedding of Prince William to Catherine Middleton in 2011 captured the attention of people around the world. The couple met while both were students at the University of St. Andrew's in Scotland, and the fact that Catherine was from an upper middle-class, non-aristocratic background made the match even more unique. Since their marriage The Duchess of Cambridge has adapted to her role with grace, charm, and dignity, and has become a highly respected member of the royal family.

For their wedding I was determined to have the best possible view of the proceedings, so I slept overnight on the ground in front of Buckingham Palace. The things we do for a good view!

I strategically chose to be near the palace and not on The Mall or near Westminster Abbey as the iconic balcony appearance was what I really wanted to see. This would take resolve and determination. To see the newly married couple with the entire royal family on the palace balcony would be *the* moment of the day. That moment was what everyone else was hoping to see as well.

I arrived with friends at 7:00 pm, the evening before to find the front-row of the processional route already filling up with crowds of jovial people. We were as ready as we could be for the long haul, carrying sleeping bags and warm clothing for the night ahead, as well as food and drink.

As the evening went on the atmosphere turned electric. The gathering crowds were singing songs, dancing in the streets, and drinking champagne. It was a time to celebrate, and people mingled among their colourful camps showing off their decorations and makeshift campsites in a spirit of friendliness and fun.

Strolling down The Mall it was delightful reading the many handmade, colourful signs attracting attention along the crowd barriers, "Check Mate Kate - You've Taken The King," "Don't Expect the Olympics to be this Good" (referring to the forthcoming 2012 London Olympics), and, "I'm holding out for Harry."

As the evening went on it was hard for people to settle down. Excitement was in the air, yet in order to save our energy for later it became necessary to try to get some rest. After a few hours of "sleep", dawn came and everyone in the crowd looked tired and dishevelled. Regardless of the exhaustion, champagne corks started popping and not long after, word circulated that The Queen had bestowed the titles of Duke and Duchess of Cambridge on the couple. At that moment someone yelled, "Three cheers for Her Majesty The Queen," and we all gave a rousing celebratory three cheers. It wasn't surprising that The Queen choose the Cambridge titles. This had been rumoured for weeks, and the speculation was reinforced when Her Majesty visited Cambridge two days prior to the wedding. It will come as no surprise that I *too* was in the crowd in Cambridge to greet her. Seeing a pattern?

By 8:00 am, the crowd size began to noticeably increase. We were being packed in whether we wanted it or not, and it soon became apparent that we wouldn't be able to move. The ability to use the facilities was a "now or never" situation. Even if you decided to move there was no guarantee you'd be allowed back into position. So there we were at 8:00 am, squashed in like sardines, in it for the duration. There was no turning back.

The morning arrivals that came by the thousands felt entitled and looked well rested. They tried relentlessly and audaciously to push in front us - yet we had camped out. They faced great opposition in us, the tired masses. We held our ground. Their bold behaviour started to enrage the determined and sleepless crowd. Angry chanting aimed at the interlopers began to get louder. There could have been a riot. To our great joy and amusement the police quickly moved these interlopers along, acknowledging the frustration felt by those of us that had claimed our positions the evening before. Crisis averted.

Having settled down, we all watched the processions heading to Westminster Abbey for the wedding service. First the family of the bride who left from The Goring Hotel, then members of the royal family left, perfectly timed in order of precedence, from Buckingham Palace. At last the bride was driven past and waived to us as she headed towards the abbey.

Everyone listened as the service was broadcast over loudspeakers. There were no smart phones at that time. The crowds sang collectively with pride during the hymns and the National Anthem. When the couple were pronounced husband and wife, the town crier sounded his bell, glasses of champagne were raised, and everyone cheered enthusiastically.

After the ceremony came the excitement and beauty of the carriage procession back to Buckingham Palace. Shoulder to shoulder in our thousands, we all surged forward to cheer the couple as they waved from the famous balcony. Calculating my position in advance, I was lucky enough to end up near the palace gates so I had a clear view as they emerged onto the balcony. This was no small feat as rows of police held back the crowds and moved us in an orderly yet unpredictable way towards the palace. I found myself crowded in by others so tightly that I couldn't move. No one could.

At last, the exciting moment was about to arrive. Until now we had only heard the wedding service and all we had seen was the couple going past in either cars or carriages, which made it difficult to see their attire. Having spent a chilly night and fought an angry crowd, we were the last people to see them! Finally they appeared. As the couple emerged onto the balcony we were all elated to see The Duke of Cambridge in his scarlet red Irish Guards Officer uniform adorned with medals, and the new duchess in her stunning wedding dress designed by Sarah Burton at fashion house Alexander McQueen. It was a day to remember.

Fast forward to the wedding of Prince Harry in 2018, and you'll discover a great contrast in how I spent the days. Both royal wedding days were special, yet I experienced them in such different ways.

In early 2018, excitement was building for the forthcoming royal wedding of Prince Harry to Meghan Markle, an American actress. It was to be held at St. George's Chapel in the Lower Ward at Windsor Castle, and there would be 600 guests inside the chapel for the ceremony. Most importantly for me, it soon became clear that additional guests would be invited to the castle that day to share in the festivities.

The official announcement read:

1,200 members of the public from every corner of the United Kingdom will be invited to Windsor Castle. They will be chosen by nine regional Lord Lieutenant offices. The couple has asked that the people chosen are from a broad range of backgrounds and ages, including young people who have shown strong leadership, and those who have served their communities.

A further 200 people from Prince Harry's charities, 100 school pupils, 610 Windsor Castle community members, and 530 members and guests of the Royal Household and Crown Estate will also get the coveted invitations.

And so it happened, much to my joy and excitement. I was one of the lucky recipients of the "coveted invitations" via the Royal Household's allocation of guests. It felt as if I had won "the golden ticket" from *Willie Wonka and the Chocolate Factory.*

I looked forward to the day with great anticipation. The printed invitation, security cards, and arrival instructions arrived in advance, and I thoroughly read over every detail. A lifetime of planning prowess readied me, as I mapped out a strategy for the big day. I chose to stay in a hotel the evening before, not far from Windsor, in Ascot.

The hotel was selected for its proximity and because it was strategically placed on the opposite side of Windsor, away from London. This was the right choice to make, as on the morning of the wedding the roads leading from London were congested, and I was chauffeured to Windsor via quiet roads.

When I arrived, the town was already buzzing with excitement. You could feel it in the air. Many people (including some that I knew) were just waking up, having spent the night along the processional route - just as I had done in 2011.

It was such fun walking along the closed streets of Windsor that were lined with thousands of people behind security barriers. As an invited guest this was something I could do, otherwise I too would have been behind the barriers along with everyone else. Amongst the crowds were people from all over the world, including a huge contingency of Americans that had flown in for the occasion.

At 8:00 am, invited guests were allowed into the castle gates. There where we were welcomed, and given a monogrammed goodie bag. Inside the bag was a printed order of service, some chocolate, a bottle of water, and a box of Scottish shortbread, as well as further printed instructions for the day. To me the jute bag itself was the best part the gift, as it featured the couple's initials and the date of the wedding. To my disbelief these bags would sell for as much as £10,000 the next day; making headline news. As a collector even I cannot imagine who would pay that much. Silliness. If you went onto eBay® today you could possibly purchase the same bag for £100!

The scene in the Lower Ward of the castle was a feast for the senses. There were fabulous hats, perfectly tailored morning suits and dresses, gorgeous floral arrangements, and countless military processions - all while beautiful prelude music was heard flowing elegantly from inside the chapel.

At Windsor Castle, 19 May 2018.

I could see all the guests arriving, like a parade passing by. Some dressed beautifully, while others perhaps could have benefited from a second opinion on their chosen attire. Among the invited guests that passed by were George and Amal Clooney, David and Victoria Beckham, Serena Williams, and Oprah Winfrey, who after the service looked over towards us and said, "Wasn't that fun?!" To which I replied, "Yes, it certainly was."

As the time came closer for the service to begin, members of the royal family began arriving; some walking, some in automobiles. Impeccably dressed in their military uniforms, when Prince Harry and The Duke of Cambridge walked past the groom looked very nervous. Every eye was on him, not only within the castle but around the world. Being nervous would be expected.

We anxiously anticipated the arrival of The Queen with The Duke of Edinburgh. Stepping out of the State Bentley we got our first glimpse of The Queen who was wearing a beautiful lime coloured coat with a matching hat trimmed in purple. I was delighted to see the duke walking so well following his hip replacement operation, which happened a few weeks earlier. The grand old duke was looking good in his morning suit, and it was wonderful to see him.

When the bride went past on her way to the west door of St. George's Chapel, she was followed by the arrival of the bridesmaids and the page boys. Prince George and Princess Charlotte were excitedly waving from inside the car. As I saw the young prince I thought to myself, "That little boy is the future king." To think that in one day I would witness four royal generations, from a 4-year-old prince and future king to his 92-year-old great grandmother the reigning monarch.

Once the service began, everyone joined along at the appropriate time in the congregational singing. We gave a rousing cheer as the couple said, "I do." Since the upper windows of the chapel were cracked open, the congregation inside heard our hearty cheer, and responded with laughter. It was a fun moment, the guests outside were communicating with the guests inside.

At certain times it was so quiet within the castle that it was easy to forget that there were hundreds of thousands of people gathered in the streets of Windsor, not to mention the 1.9 billion watching the proceedings via television. Despite the considerable numbers, for those of us within the castle, the day still had an intimate "family wedding" feel.

For a royal event, I found there to be a few unconventional moments, such as the long-winded and over-the-top address by the American Bishop, Michael Curry. It was also unusual hearing a gospel choir singing *This Little Light of Mine* as the service concluded. During this boisterous postlude I watched as members of the royal family interacted with each other as they exited the chapel. As has been the case throughout their marriage, the couple have their *own way* of doing things.

The weather that day could not have been better. Clear blue skies and sunshine added to the feeling of being a part of something special, and those of us within the castle walls had been shown great hospitality - royal hospitality. Luckily, royal hospitality has been extended to me on many occasions. These events add such a splash of colour to life.

***

I have always been drawn to Westminster Abbey, the setting for royal weddings as well as countless other events of state. Some of the most memorable moments in my own life have taken place within the ancient walls.

During the summer of 2011, after Prince William's wedding, I heard that a service would take place at Westminster Abbey to commemorate the 400th anniversary of the King James Bible. Scheduled for later in the year, without hesitation I contacted the King James Bible Trust, asking for an invitation. I was interested in attending as I knew The Queen would be the guest of honour that day.

It was right and fitting that the service would take place at Westminster, for it was in the Jerusalem Chamber in 1611 that the final editing of the Authorised Version of the King James Bible occurred.

I arrived at the abbey at 9:15 am, hoping to be the first one in the security queue, and sure enough I was. Never one to underestimate the power of arriving early, I knew that doing this would increase my chances for being seated in a prime location. The doors opened at 10:00 am, and I was the first guest to enter the abbey.

When I arrived at my seating section, I quicky noted the thrones where The Queen, The Duke of Edinburgh, and The Prince of Wales would be seated. I still wasn't sure of the location of my seat so I asked the usher for assistance. She said, "Oh, you're the first one here, so let's see... ah... you should sit right here," pointing to a chair in the second row within five feet of The Queen's throne. I couldn't believe it! How could that seat not be reserved for a VIP? This was my chance, and it was being offered, so I thanked her and sat down as quickly as I could. I kept thinking that there must have been a mistake. How could it be possible that I would be afforded the privilege to sit so close to The Queen? Would I be moved by an usher to make way for a long lost or forgotten VIP? I wasn't.

It was time for the service to begin. The vast space was filled with the sounds of a trumpet fanfare announcing The Queen as she began her procession down the main aisle of the ancient abbey.

A few moments later, The Queen, The Duke of Edinburgh, and The Prince of Wales slowly approached. As they passed by in procession, I gave them a neck bow, and could not believe, here I was, seated within a few feet of them. I thought, "Is this really happening?" I pinched myself.

Later, The Duke of Edinburgh whispered what must have been a joke to Prince Charles, while Her Majesty retrieved something from her handbag. My eyes were glued to the goings on as she pulled out... her glasses.

What an occasion it was, yet over the years I've spent many special days *inside*, as well as *outside* Westminster Abbey. It was outside in the cold pouring rain on 20 November 2007, that I stood to see The Queen and The Duke of Edinburgh following the Service of Thanksgiving for their 60th Wedding Anniversary.

It was a much dryer occasion inside the abbey on 15 October 2019, when I attended a service to celebrate the 750th anniversary of the rebuilding of Westminster Abbey.

My friend Ian Shapiro accompanied me on this occasion and when we arrived at the abbey that morning, it was the age-old standing in the queue and wondering if the guests in front of us would be better placed once inside the abbey. Of course, I recognised a few of the faces lining up with us.

When the queue started to move we went through security, and once inside, walked up the centre aisle towards the transept. Based on my earlier abbey experience I knew where the guests of honour would be seated, so I was keen to be in that area again. Rather like déjà vu we were permitted to sit in one of the unallocated seats next to where the royal party would be.

Looking thru the order of service I was delighted to read that so much beautiful music would be included. Hymns such as *The Church's One Foundation* as well as prelude music by Henry Purcell, the organist of Westminster Abbey between 1679-1695, and by Orlando Gibbons, organist between 1623-1625.

Anticipation was building. I punctuated the moment, consciously looking down at my watch. It was 11:20 am, and the abbey bells began pealing out in celebration. Everyone started singing *Christ is Made the Sure Foundation* and on the third verse the procession of Her Majesty The Queen, and The Duchess of Cornwall came into view. As The Queen passed by, everyone in our seating area were on-point with neck bows and deep curtsies.

Abigail Wallace, the Chaplain of The Queen's Scholars, was standing next to The Queen's chair holding a bouquet of beautiful red roses. The roses, a tribute from The Queen, were to be laid on the altar in the Shrine of Edward the Confessor. Her Majesty touched the bouquet, signifying them as her personal gift. They were then taken into the shrine.

A prayer was said for Queen Elizabeth I, who had issued a royal charter to The College of St. Peter at Westminster in 1560. At that very moment, I realised that I was looking at Queen Elizabeth II who was sitting in the very spot where both were crowned queen - 394 years apart. It was a powerful moment, and a reminder of the breadth of history and tradition that had occurred within the abbey walls.

Sounds of a triumphant organ postlude announced the conclusion of the service. Uplifting and dramatic, the pipes were soon joined by the pealing of bells, which could be heard throughout Westminster.

Before leaving I looked over and noticed St. Edward's Chair, famously known as The Coronation Chair. In this ancient seat British kings and queens have been anointed with holy oil, received the regalia, and crowned for their lofty place in the pages of history. Seeing the chair I smiled, as I knew I had just experienced another small moment in the rich history of both Westminster Abbey and the monarchy. For me, that day was more than just a royal encounter, it was an encounter with history.

Chapter Seven:
"The World is Your Oyster"

"Travel is fatal to prejudice, bigotry, and narrow-mindedness, and many of our people need it sorely on these accounts. Broad, wholesome, charitable views of men and things cannot be acquired by vegetating in one little corner of the earth all one's lifetime."
– Mark Twain

In my view, truer words have not been written. The greatest education I have ever received is found amongst the pages of my passport. Travel is vital to a soul like mine. Enjoying new experiences, making memories, and turning "those people" into friends can be so rewarding. Over the years I have been fortunate enough to do a great deal of travelling, and as you will see, not just in the United Kingdom.

My love of travel has taken me around the world. From Asia to Africa, India to Australia, my pursuit of travel and far-off adventures has offered me many unique experiences. And the older I become the more I appreciate the exotic locations. The places that expose you to culture shock stick with you the longest, or at least that has been my experience.

"The only rule in India is that there are no rules"

So said my local guide not long after my arrival.

Nothing can prepare you for India and specifically for Old Town Delhi. The sights, smells, colours, and stimulation are unforgettable and can become for some - addictive. The intensity of extremes is not for everyone. Upon arrival India is initially exhausting, especially for the first-time visitor. Exhaustion can become enchantment when you open your mind to experience the life being lived at every turn.

The country provides a feast for the senses, and still to this day I have never felt more alive than when I was in India. Senses immediately go into overdrive. Walking through the streets I was thinking, "This is the most beautiful thing I've ever seen," and the next second, "Oh my, that is *horrendous*." These extremes were punctuated by the reality of two cows and four tuk-tuks about to run me down while I attempted to cross yet another chaotic street teaming with traffic. India was constant, persistent, in your face stimulation. Once you get used to it (and you do) some people can actually thrive on the energy. That is exactly what happened to me.

The glory of seeing the Taj Mahal for the first time took me by surprise. This magnificent example of Mughal architecture was commissioned in 1632 by the Mughal emperor Shah Jahan. It was built to house the tomb of his favourite wife Mumtaz Mahal, who died at the age of 38. Today it is seen as a monument to eternal love.

As I travelled to Agra, I felt like I was going to see something that I was *expected to see*. Going was "the thing to do", so when I got there, to my complete astonishment it was more spectacular than I could have ever imagined. Walking through the gateway facing the Taj Mahal, my jaw dropped, and I said out loud with a voice of awe, "Oh my word." It is justifiably a Wonder of the World, and my being filled with such wonder was totally unexpected that morning. Visiting the Taj Mahal was one of the great moments of my life.

Touring Rashtrapati Bhavan was another highlight of my trip. In 1911, when India was under British rule, the capital of India moved from Calcutta to New Delhi. Sir Edwin Lutyens, the renowned English architect, drafted the designs and construction started on the complex in 1912. It was to be an official residence for the Viceroy of India, as well as the centrepiece of New Delhi.

At the Taj Mahal (Top) and Arriving to the Amber Fort near Jaipur (Bottom) September 2018.

Today Rashtrapati Bhavan serves as the Official Residence of the President of India. On the grounds are the beautiful Mughal Gardens, where Mahatma Gandhi and Lord Mountbatten then the Viceroy of India met to iron out the process of transition from British rule to independence. Despite their great differences, through these conversations they ultimately established a level of trust and mutual respect for one another.

One day on the outskirts of Delhi, I stood in a large rundown park filled with tall weeds and unkept bushes. The location was the site for the 1911 Delhi Durbar which was an imperial ceremony to recognise King George V & Queen Mary as Emperor and Empress of India. I could imagine the one-time splendour of this mass assembly. Images and newsreels of the elaborate durbar show the Indian rulers paying their homage. Standing on the spot where the royal dais stood, I could imagine resplendent maharajas, the British contingent, and the many thousands that gathered on that day. Mine was a vision of a bygone era.

Later in my trip I spent a good deal of time in Jaipur, the capital city of Rajasthan. I found it to be an architectural delight with its maharajah palaces, and the iconic Amber Fort. I made a grand entrance to the fort atop an elephant, I am pleased to say.

My chauffeur Gurvinder became my constant companion as we navigated the long drives in and out of Delhi. He met me in the lobby of my hotel in Old Town Delhi one morning before sunrise to walk me to his car nearby. Outside it was still dark, and as we left the hotel we had to step over people sleeping on the steps. Walking together in the dark, the early morning call to prayer could be heard from the mosque and men were curled up and sleeping on the seats of their rickshaws.

As our walk continued I observed a child that should be asleep, bathing in a large puddle of dirty water instead. Mischievous monkeys maximised every moment to seize remnants from the quiet streets. This early morning walk remains etched in my mind.

On our last day together I donned a turban (as is customary) and Gurvinder gave me a tour of his temple. He took great pride in explaining Sikhism, and the way he tried to live out his faith every day. I observed the enormous soup kitchen that serves meals to 20,000 impoverished people every day, and I was treated to the experience of sitting on the floor with countless others, awaiting my turn to partake in the teatime meal being served. I felt as if I was talking a meal from someone who really needed it. Gurvinder sensed my hesitation and said, "All who come to the temple are special and should be fed."

Gurvinder and I before we toured his temple.

These are the moments that remain. In my mind, I can still see a little boy playing along the Ganges River. I recall looking at the water with horror as sewage, garbage, and ashes floated along, pouring out from the crematorium on the opposite side of the river. The small boy looked at me, waved with great enthusiasm, and jumped into the water splashing. He was having the time of his life.

Reacting from a western point of view, I thought to myself, "Get out of that dirty water." I then stopped and realised that nothing about this was unusual in India. I looked at him again, heard his laughter, and quickly saw the fun that he was having. This was simply a child being a child. It was a powerful reminder that we need to stop and enjoy life no matter our circumstances. For he was making the most of his situation, and his life, in *extraordinary* India.

"You'll be seeing a lot of breasts today"

Our tour director smiled mischievously as he said this.

We were on a coach driving down dusty backroads in South Africa. Such an announcement naturally created a huge amount of awkward laughter. We were about to arrive at a Zulu village when I quickly realised the truth of those words. Upon arrival we were led on a walk around the village. It felt like show and tell. Whisking off their colourful upper garments the unmarried girls were freely showing "their wares." It all happened so fast! Later we were told they were looking for husbands.

Not long afterwards it became apparent that the locals had a homemade beer they wanted us to try. The thought crossed my mind, "What a perfect opportunity for them to get rid of me." In order not to offend I smiled and took a very small drink of the Zulu beer. It didn't taste too bad actually. My entire time in Zululand in KwaZulu-Natal province, and indeed throughout South Africa was just as eye-opening.

The journey continued into the Kingdom of Swaziland (now Eswatini) for a few days, then back into South Africa culminating in three wonderful days on safari in Kruger National Park. This vast area is one of the largest reserves in Africa covering 7,523 square miles. Enjoying an African safari in an open jeep is, in my mind, one of life's great experiences. Nothing can prepare you for turning the corner in the bush only to encounter enormous herds of elephant and giraffe dotted across the open African landscape. While on safari everyone's goal is to see the "Big Five" - elephants, lions, African buffalo, rhinos, and leopards. The safari experience feels timeless, yet every day conservationists work hard to preserve these fragile ecosystems so that they exist for others to enjoy in the future. A task made more daunting given the mistreatment and poaching of animals in the wild. I viewed the gravity of the situation while visiting a rhino preserve.

Shockingly, because the rhino tusk is so valuable, each rhino had an around-the-clock armed bodyguard standing by to protect it.

The cheetah is well-known as the fastest animal in the World, capable of reaching speeds of up to 70 miles per hour. At a cheetah rehabilitation centre, we were admiring two of these magnificent creatures from the outside of a large fenced-in area. Then the tour director proclaimed, "We're all going to go into the pen to pet the cheetah." My response was, "Like hell we are." In my mind I had immediately imagined that everyone in the tour group looked like lunch to the cheetahs. Oh well, you only live once, so we proceeded with apprehension and silent caution into their domain. One cheetah was lying on the grass and allowed us to queue up for a careful "cuddle." All the while, the second beast paced back and forth around us, never taking his eyes off the situation. I watched as each person in the group stepped forward to pet the cheetah, after which everyone remained intact. Finally, it was my turn. My heart raced as I stepped up to the beast. I suspect it was the fastest I have ever touched anything in my life, but I did it none the less, and lived to tell the tale.

South Africa is a land of extremes. Just outside of Johannesburg, I remember seeing a shantytown on one side of a road and a Louis Vuitton store, complete with armed guards at the door, on the other. Similar contrasts are reflected in the variety of the terrain. The landscape is varied and changes quickly, from rugged hills one moment to flat bushlands the next, and from palm fringed beaches to the chill waters in the South Atlantic Ocean. Standing high atop Table Mountain looking down at beautiful Cape Town, I was reminded of how small a place we occupy on this earth, and how much we can be rewarded if we make the effort to go that extra mile. As I have often discovered, the extra mile is the most rewarding mile.

"I've never seen water hit those windows before!"

Those are not the words you want to hear from a bartender aboard the *Queen Mary 2* in the middle of the North Atlantic.

At that moment I was attempting to enjoy a drink in Commodore Club. The transatlantic voyage had already been rocky, but it became much worse as we started to hit stormy, 30 foot waves. The Commodore Club is an elegant lounge with large windows facing the ship's bow. Positioned all the way up on Deck 9 of the *QM2*, the club normally sits high above the sea. The waves were so enormous that water was splashing on the windows, more than 80 feet above the waterline, as the ocean liner navigated into a huge storm.

At that hour of the day the club should have been filled with guests enjoying their pre-dinner drink. Instead, most of the passengers were in their rooms, probably looking green, being ill, or both. But for whatever reason, despite being raised in land-locked Indiana, I have very good sea legs. Despite the extreme motion I decided to soldier on up to Deck 9 and head to the bar. As I sipped on my gin martini, the bartender's aforementioned observation about the water hitting the windows received my rather sarcastic reply, "Thank you. How very reassuring."

In the library aboard Queen Mary 2.

Aboard Queen Mary 2.

A funeral procession down the Grand Canal

Venice, glorious Venice, is a place that cannot be fully described. It must be experienced in-person to appreciate why it has captured the imagination of artists, poets, writers, and tourists for centuries. The beauty of it has completely captured my imagination ever since my first visit in 2006.

On my inaugural visit I arrived at the train station, transferred onto a vaporetto, and began the iconic journey down the Grand Canal. The vaporetti are Venice's public transport, boats that travel down the canals making frequent stops throughout the city. They are rather like city buses - yet on the water.

While on the vaporetto I was taken by the beautiful sight of a funeral procession of gondolas as they processed down the Grand Canal. On the first gondola was a coffin lying on a bed of roses. Just behind was another, filled with Italian women in long black dresses with mourning veils of lace covering their faces. It felt as if I had stepped back in time and into a Canaletto painting. My love for Venice was sealed right then.

Since that first trip, I have returned to Venice almost yearly. The city never fails to charm and delight with its beautiful art, renowned architecture, and fabulous cuisine. I am especially fond of the elegance of Fortuny fabrics, still produced in a variety of vivid and timeless Venetian patterns in their Giudecca workshop.

Venice is often overrun with tourists, but in some neighbourhoods and during certain times of the year it can be quiet and peaceful. Some of my favourite haunts can be found among the charming squares and side streets along the Giudecca Canal. As a frequent visitor I have viewed first-hand how vulnerable the city is to rising sea levels. Being in Venice during the Acqua Alta (high water) is a sobering experience. To see centuries old mosaics in St. Mark's Basilica under water, and to walk at every turn on platforms raised to avoid the flooding, reminds one of the city's fragility.

One dinner in Venice sticks out in my mind. How could it not since the restaurant flooded during the meal?! An unexpected hailstorm caused the canal waters to rise, enter the restaurant, and cover the floor. We had to dine with our legs folded up on our chairs until the water eventually receded. The entire time our waiters continued sludging through the cloudy water. The food still came out, the wine continued to flow, and the Venetian staff just got on with things - in typical Italian fashion.

From the opulence of the Doge's Palace to the magnificence of the Rialto Bridge, it is easy to marvel at one of the world's most beautiful cities. Today just as ever Venice is a wonder to behold, built centuries ago - rising majestically out of a lagoon.

"Iceland in January was wonderful"

I usually get a strange look when I say that to people.

January in Iceland was incredible. So much so, that I went back a second time, also in January, to uncover the many winter wonders of this proud island nation. If you have been to Reykjavík, you will know it is a charming place. To see Iceland's capital city in the snow is a bonus. In the city centre geothermal pipes underneath the streets melt the snow and ice, so they rarely need to use snow ploughs or chemicals to clear the roads. This is very ingenious, as well as environmentally friendly.

From time-to-time I am keen to get in the saddle - especially on my travels. The Icelandic Horse are a breed that I had read about, so what better time than in January to "have a go" at riding this magnificent small creature? They are work horses that look like ponies and soldier on no matter the weather, this makes them ideal for the extremes of Iceland. During my ride the weather turned into a small blizzard. The horse and I managed well despite this unfortunate turn of events, and we both returned to the stables looking cold and dishevelled.

The highlight of any trip to Iceland during the winter season is seeing the Northern Lights, which is not a given. Already on my bucket list, I booked a late-night tour departure from Reykjavík. This involved being driven out into the middle of nowhere, far outside of the city, and staring into a clear and star filled sky, hoping to catch a glimpse of the renowned cosmic display. A good supply of patience is required, as reflected in my journal entries:

"Night one: Depart Reykjavík at 21:30, Return at 2:00. Beautiful stars tonight. Frigid temperature."

"Night two: Depart Reykjavík at 21:30, Return at 2:35. Spotted a gorgeous moon tonight."

"Night three: Depart Reykjavík at 21:30, Return at 1:45. Success at last!"

To see the Aurora Borealis on the third evening, if only for a matter of moments, was well-worth the effort. The ethereal fluorescent green dancing through the sky in a whirlwind was a feast for the eyes, and something a photograph could not begin to capture.

With minimal daylight and cold temperatures in January, meals are the perfect time to warm up in Iceland. The lobster soup there became a favourite, as did the local salmon, which is the freshest I have ever eaten. Due to Iceland's location in the middle of the North Atlantic, they import almost everything so high-quality food and drinks tend to be expensive. This reality hit home when enjoying a basic cup of coffee for 1,000 ISK ($7.00 USD). Luckily, the coffee was delicious!

"There is nothing to see here"

The elderly Maltese woman yelled at me, leaning out of her window as I stood on the street below.

I ignored her, in reality there was much to see, and I had read all about the woman that was yelling. Villa Guardamangia in Valletta, Malta was the home of Princess Elizabeth and Philip, Duke of Edinburgh in the early 1950s. Despite its historic significance as a much-loved former royal residence, in the years after their departure the villa had fallen into disrepair. Everyone knew that the owner allowed this to happen. She was keen to sell it to redevelopers that were interested in building residential flats. She often slammed the door on visitors and members of the press when they arrived, usually wanting to know why she refused to maintain the property. I left that trip to Malta feeling disappointed, knowing it was only a matter of time before the villa would be lost forever. However when I returned in 2019, it was a new day. The owner had passed away and the villa was up for sale.

Upon my return to Valletta, after the death of the owner, I heard that there had been an auction. Throwing my collector's hat on, I thought of how wonderful it would be to own something that had formerly been in the villa. So the search commenced. I spent an entire day combing the streets of Valletta determined to find something sold in the auction. Approaching numerous antique dealers I asked each the same question, "Did you purchase anything from the Villa Guardamangia auction?" "No," was the frequent answer. Finally I stumbled across a shop tucked away in a narrow alley. As I entered I noticed a table with a small label that read "Villa Guardamangia", it also contained the name of the auction house and the date of the sale. EUREKA!

I approached the shopkeeper and asked, "The small table from Villa Guardamangia, is it for sale?" Sadly it was already sold, but I inquired if he knew of any other items that had come out of the villa. He did, and connected me with a gentleman who had purchased a large gilt mirror that had once hung above the mantle in the main drawing room. We made arrangements to meet, and I was driven to a small village outside of Valletta. The mirror was just what I was hoping to find, so I bought it and had it shipped to England in a large custom-made crate. Further research has proven that the mirror, which now hangs in my home, had been in the villa for many years.

Today, Heritage Malta has taken on the monumental task of restoring the villa and plans to open it as a museum. I look forward to returning to see Villa Guardamangia, beautiful once again. At that time I will be able say, along with many other visitors, "Yes, there certainly IS something to see here."

At Villa Guardamangia in Malta, September 2019.

"You've met MY queen six times and you're not even BLOODY BRITISH?!"

The indignant British woman loudly exclaimed while slamming her hands on the elegantly laid table, jostling the plates and the silver, and all of us seated around.

Everything stopped and everyone laughed, then all eyes turned to see my reaction. Without hesitation I straightened up in my chair, puffed out my chest, and haughtily confirmed, "Yes, and I'll take *you* to meet her as well." If first impressions were anything, that comment should have put me off. Instead, it did just the opposite. I admired Maggie's feistiness from the start, and ever since that dinner aboard the *Queen Elizabeth 2* we have been friends. Maggie and I remained table companions throughout that final westbound transatlantic crossing of the *QE2* in October 2008.

The cruise sold-out in under 15 minutes, more than a year and a half before this historic final crossing. The most famous ocean liner in the world was set to be decommissioned by Cunard, so it was a "now or never" opportunity. Sailing across the Atlantic in tandem with the *Queen Mary 2*, both ships sailed out of Southampton and arrived 6.5 days later to New York amid great fanfare. The celebration continued throughout the day culminating with fireworks that evening over the Statue of Liberty.

After our shared voyage I kept my word to Maggie and took her to see The Queen during a walkabout in Bury St. Edmunds, which followed the Royal Maundy service. Though heavily pregnant, Maggie even joined me to camp out overnight in front of Buckingham Palace during the 2011 royal wedding. We also enjoyed events together during The Queen's Diamond Jubilee in 2012. Whenever I invite her to join me for a unique royal experience, I recall my first encounter with this blunt, red haired woman. I've been known to tease her by saying, "You see, and I'm not even BLOODY BRITISH."

Sunrise over Victoria Harbour

Hong Kong is a captivating place. East meets West in such a vibrant way. Countless chic towers, constantly changing due to the light, reach up amongst forested mountains. Civilisation springing out of nature surrounds this busy, bustling commercial harbour. Redolent in history and culturally complex, Hong Kong doesn't fail to capture the imagination. Experiencing it's vibrance today makes it nearly impossible to think back to the time of Queen Victoria's reign when the harbour was a remote British outpost. Amongst bustling towers are enduring reminders of Hong Kong's past, including the Star Ferry, The Victoria Prison, The Old Supreme Court, and St. John's Cathedral.

I am not a morning person. If I must, by choice, get up early I am either heading to a train station, to an airport, or perhaps to take part in an auction. Many of my tour guests are relieved when they realise that crack-of-dawn starts to the daily agenda are rare. So for me to get up to see the sunrise, it must be extraordinary.

The Ritz Carlton Kowloon is situated across Victoria Harbour from the Sheung Wan and Central neighbourhoods, and the hotel has a renowned glass-walled restaurant on the 103rd floor. On my last day in Hong Kong I decided to get up early to see the sunrise from the restaurant and take in the view. Endless towers lit the darkened sky until the vibrant sunrise appeared, and suddenly the day was upon us. From my vantage point high above the harbour, I watched the city emerge from the darkness into the light. The colours of the day revealed enormous ships and the city streets as they bustled into life. At that moment, from this amazing view my window on the world was fascinating, stunning, and remains etched in my mind.

"Up, Up and Away"

These were the words of the hot air balloon pilot as we lifted off over the Hunter Valley just outside of Sydney, Australia.

Rising early, I hesitated briefly that morning since the cloud cover was significant. I wanted to realise my dream of riding in a hot air balloon. Would the cloud cover obscure my view and dampen my experience? I had to be at the launch site at 4:30 am, you may recall I am not a morning person. This was our second endeavour, the day before was a failed attempt.

Lifting off there was a quiet calm. As we gained elevation the world below was getting smaller and smaller, and it began to feel like an out of body experience. Then we burst through the clouds, and I saw something remarkable - a glorious dawn. There it was - the bright morning sun. Right in front of me as we emerged from the clouds. So close, I could have touched them - dazzling colours, subtly changing by the second. It was magical.

Our silent voyage was tranquil. It was calm. It was serene - yet surreal.

The clouds began to break as we floated over hills, vineyards, and the beautiful Blue Mountains. During the descent, one of my favourite quotes by Oscar Wilde came to mind, "To live is the rarest thing in the world."

A glorious sight bursting through the clouds while in the hot air balloon.

"Come, sit and have lunch with my family"

So said the Turkish carpet seller as I was about to leave his shop.

Buying a Turkish rug in Istanbul had been on my bucket list for as long as I can remember. I had done my research, what to look for, what questions to ask, and I was prepared to barter on the price as is customary in Turkey. I selected the rug all the while being plied with coffee and lokum - real Turkish Delight. The decision was made, the price agreed upon, and our exchange was over…or so I thought.

Before I could leave the shop I was beckoned back. "Have you had lunch?" asked the shopkeeper. At first I brushed it off with, "Oh, I'll find something nearby." To which he responded, "No, no. Please join us. Come, sit and have lunch with my family." It was an offer I couldn't refuse.

He motioned me to the rear of the shop which opened into their family dining room. The white walls were filled with photographs and Nazar Boncuk Charms (Turkish Eye Beads), but no table in sight. On the floor was a huge, colourful Turkish carpet on which I was invited to sit cross-legged with everyone else. A variety of food was soon paraded in to join us on the carpet - meats, hummus, breads, dips, and other mouth-watering delights. It was apparent that each dish was lovingly prepared. My host's family were all very eager to show me kindness and hospitality, both of which I soaked up with the delicious food.

As I left, the rug seller said to me, "I hope you now have a good memory to go along with your rug." "I certainly do," I replied. Little did they know that they had just made my birthday even more special.

"This blessed plot..."

Of all the countries I've been fortunate enough to visit, only one personifies me, and is part and parcel to my identity. One place that combines my passion for heritage and tradition with my desire for variety and excitement - the United Kingdom. I am always amazed how one small island can offer so much.

Many of my British friends say that I have seen more of the country than they have, and that is very likely the case. You'll find me on a train crossing the country to explore old favourites and discovering new gems whenever possible. Sitting still has never been my strong suit.

From the magic of London to the tranquillity of the Cotswolds, from the splendours of the Highlands to the many beautiful villages dotted around the West Country, and from the Giant's Causeway to the wonders of Wales - the United Kingdom is a spectacular place.

From Land's End to John o' Groats and everything in between, to know Britain is to love her. Her proud and stately traditions make for a charming place to visit. Or to call home.

> *This royal throne of kings, this sceptred isle,*
> *This earth of majesty, this seat of Mars,*
> *This other Eden, demi-paradise,*
> *This fortress built by Nature for herself*
> *Against infection and the hand of war,*
> *This happy breed of men, this little world,*
> *This precious stone set in the silver sea,*
> *Which serves it in the office of a wall*
> *Or as a moat defensive to a house,*
> *Against the envy of less happier lands,*
> *This blessed plot, this earth, this realm, this England.*

-William Shakespeare, "King Richard II"

Chapter Eight: "You're Still Here!"

It was 20 March 2015 and His Royal Highness The Prince of Wales and The Duchess of Cornwall were visiting Louisville, Kentucky to recognise the city's sustainability efforts. Their official tour of the United States also included visits to The White House and to George Washington's home at Mount Vernon. Louisville was just over an hour's drive from my Indianapolis home, so I decided to make the effort to drive down - how could I not since royalty rarely came to me. There were five engagements planned for the day. Having researched in advance I knew I could be near three of the engagements based on their timing and location.

The first two were failed attempts. The streets were cordoned off for the first engagement and for the second I was only able to get a fleeting glimpse from hundreds of yards away. The US Secret Service kept the public at such a distance that views of the royal party were nearly impossible. Security in the United States surrounding members of the royal family is obstructive compared to these types of royal visits within the United Kingdom. As The Queen once said, "I have to be seen to be believed."

It was starting to feel like a total loss. Yet, I had one last chance to salvage the day. His Royal Highness was scheduled to give a major speech on environmental sustainability, so off I went to the Cathedral of the Assumption in downtown Louisville. Being a seasoned royal watcher, I noted the crowd barriers at the side of the cathedral. "Ah ha, this will be the entrance he will use," I thought to myself. All indications were that the prince's arrival would take place shortly near the spot where I was standing.

Not long after, the car conveying The Prince of Wales pulled up - just as I had hoped. Out stepped Prince Charles who walked right over to me and a few of the others waiting, shook our hands, and offered a few nice sentiments. To my amusement, and in his usual style he asked, "Have you been waiting long?"

Then the Prince went into the cathedral to deliver his speech. The crowd mostly dissipated, but I waited and stood in place for the next hour - hoping for another glimpse of his departure. My perseverance was rewarded as he came out of the cathedral, pointed directly at me and said, "You're *still* here!"

My reply, "Yes, Your Royal Highness, I am *still* here."

The Louisville Courier-Journal captured the moment.

His playful remark pretty much summarises my dedication when seeing members of the royal family in person. So why do I do it? What exactly is it that drives me to go to such lengths?

It all goes back to the importance of curating an experience. It is not enough to read about The Queen, or other members of the royal family - or to even collect royal objects of note. I cherish the experience and memories associated with these royal events. Yes, taking a photograph is nice, but a quick personal interaction is better and where exceptional memories are made.

In the years since there have been many interactions with The Prince of Wales and The Duchess of Cornwall, but the evening of 2 July 2019, would turn out to be the best of the best. My written account of the evening sets the scene:

Driving down rural, tree lined lanes, with wild hedges. Finally, you reach it. The only markings are signs that read "LW", standing for Llwynywermod, which translates in English to, "a grove of Wormwoods."

A royal residence nestled in the heart of Wales. Hidden on the edge of the Brecon Beacons. The Welsh sanctuary, and base of a prince and his duchess when in this noble principality. Once parked in a field of green grass, we walk down a tree lined path. On my left I see a stunning claret helicopter sitting stationary in a wild, yet beautiful grassy field. Then I see equally beautiful buildings set down in a valley with an inviting path to walk down. As I proceed, there is something simply magical - a field of tall grass and wildflowers which not only pleases the eye but must surely provide a haven for so many different species. This visual feast personifies the current Prince of Wales and his approach to organic and responsible farming and agriculture.

I descend the path and approach a building. It may only be a whitewashed stone barn, but thoughts immediately turn to elegance. Inside the barn - the floors are covered in fine and varied hand-woven carpets in various shapes and colours. I see a gilded harp featuring the carved feathers of the Prince of Wales - one that is usually kept in the Morning Room at Clarence House. In addition, there is a royal coat of arms set into the stone wall, just behind where the musicians will perform. A reminder that this barn is far from ordinary.

A cool summer breeze flows alongside the summer evening sound of birdsong. Then Their Royal Highnesses, The Prince of Wales and The Duchess of Cornwall, arrive and sit in the row in front of me. As they enter, smiles abound, and hushed pleasantries are exchanged.

As the performance begins, this oasis is filled with the sound of fine Welsh music from instruments of all types - including the male and female voice. In addition to the beautiful music, there are hilarious moments of laughter shared by all. There is also puppetry, poetry, and drama.

Throughout the performance, a gorgeous summer evening shows its variety and beauty - from chickens walking gently past the door, to a lovely bird flying from beam to beam above my head. I look upwards to admire the beautiful oak hammerbeam roof.

My seat behind the future king provides a bonus to what is already a most intimate experience.

At the conclusion of the performance, there is the debut of the newly announced Official Harpist to The Prince of Wales, Alis Huws. Later in the evening, I chat with her as she radiates with pride at her new posting. Her family and tutor are there as well, and the excitement and joy she feels is shared with all who speak with her during the evening.

Guests mingle over champagne while Their Royal Highnesses greeted the cast of performers. Then they begin to engage with the other guests.

As The Prince of Wales approached he extended his hand, and I offered my hand in return, with a neck bow. The conversation included the gardens at Llwynywermod (which looked stunning), and the conservation and restoration of Gwrych Castle in North Wales.

At Llwynywermod with The Prince of Wales - 2 July 2019.

A few moments later, I mentioned to His Royal Highness that I had been looking through the Christie's catalogues of Dumfries House - an auction which never happened due to his personal intervention. This incredible Scottish collection was scheduled to be sold by Christie's in 2007 until he stepped in to save it for the nation. The magnificent rooms at Dumfries House include an outstanding collection of 18th Century furniture by Thomas Chippendale - all of which had never left the estate. I told him, "I want to commend you for stepping in to save the collection at Dumfries." And he replied with, "Thank you. Can you imagine if it had been disbanded?" He continued, "Have you been to see it?" To which I responded, "Yes, and I'm going again soon." With great delight he said, "Well done!"

A conversation with the future king.

As the party continued, I stepped out into the beautiful courtyard garden. It looked like a dream. Gorgeous soft-colour flowers, low evening sunlight, and the sound of a gentle fountain. It was as if nature was putting on a show for the guests.

A few minutes later, the Duchess of Cornwall approached, and we enjoyed a nice conversation covering various topics such as the development of the house, and their hectic schedule during their time in Wales. She said, "I wish we could come down more often." She continued to share that she was looking forward to the time ahead in Scotland as she would be able to spend time with her grandchildren at Birkhall, their residence in the Highlands.

During the performance there had been puppetry, including a skinny cat puppet which looked like a skeleton with enormous eyes. I asked her what she thought of it and she said, "Did you see its horrible eyes bulging out?" over which we had a little giggle. I gently teased, "Anyone would run a mile if that cat appeared in the dark."

She moved on by asking me what I do, and I shared, "I own a tour company and put together country house, castle, and garden tours." She responded, "Oh how lovely," and I continued, "I've taken a few of my groups to the gardens at Highgrove," her residence in Gloucestershire - which delighted her.

Since the conversation was going very well, I decided to show my cards a bit and say, "I thought I would mention that over the years, we've had some correspondence." She replied inquisitively, "Oh really?" "Yes," I responded, "and I've always appreciated that you've sent a personal reply." She shared earnestly, "I think if someone takes the trouble to write a kind note, they should receive a personal reply from me." Asking my name, she makes the connection, "Oh yes! Andrew from America. You have been so kind to me over the years. How nice to put a name to a face."

A few other pleasantries were exchanged, but by that point in the evening their royal highnesses were at the reception 15 minutes after their expected departure time. She ended our conversation with, "How nice to have officially met you."

Later, walking through the wildflower meadow, I knew I just had a very special experience. It was simply magical.

There were just a handful of guests that evening, and I suspect we all left with the feeling we had just experienced something very special. It was yet another reminder that the royal family is in the "happiness business." And few events epitomise this business more than the annual summer garden parties hosted by Her Majesty.

Summer garden parties at Buckingham Palace originated during the reign of Queen Victoria (1837-1901). Originally the guests invited were debutantes or members of the aristocracy. In the 1950s, the present queen expanded these events so she could meet many different types of people from a more representative range of society. Today guests are invited from within the United Kingdom, the Commonwealth, and even from the wider world.

An invitation to Her Majesty's garden parties cannot be applied for, making it a most exclusive invite. Many who attend the garden parties have achieved something great within their community. An invite might also be recognition for a lifetime of volunteering or acknowledgement for outstanding leadership in the community.

Each summer four garden parties take place, three at Buckingham Palace in London, and one at the Palace of Holyroodhouse which is The Queen's official residence in Edinburgh, Scotland. You can imagine my reaction when in 2017 I received an invitation to the 1 June 2017 garden party at Buckingham Palace. This was tremendously exciting, and I was determined to make it a day to remember.

I carefully planned my attire which included a new suit and new shoes, as well as two cherished pieces from my collection which properly "fit the bill" for such a special day. I chose to wear a pair of gold and enamel royal presentation cufflinks, and a diamond and platinum pin, both of which feature Her Majesty's EIIR cypher.

The garden party didn't begin until the afternoon, so I had plenty of time for a civilised lunch at The Wolseley, followed by a men's grooming session at the legendary Truefitt & Hill. Truefitt & Hill is the oldest barber shop in the world, and famously looks after The Duke of Edinburgh and The Prince of Wales, as well as other male members of the royal family; historic clientele included Winston Churchill, Oscar Wilde, Laurence Olivier, and Frank Sinatra. With not a single hair out of place, it was time to head to the palace.

As usual there were large crowds milling outside of the palace. It was hard not to have my head held high as I walked past the many tourists with my invitation in hand. Naturally those of us that were "all dressed up" were of interest to the onlookers gathering at the palace gates.

It was exciting walking across the forecourt of the palace, under the famous balcony, and up the red carpeted stairs into the grand entrance. I was greeted with, "Good afternoon. Welcome," by a liveried footman.

Once in the garden, I *marvelled* in the moment.

I enjoyed a leisurely stroll over the lawn and towards the famous Waterloo Vase. Just past the vase, which is enormous in size, is The Queen's Rose Garden featuring a lovely small summer house and many filled rose beds - all elegantly laid out. Over the years, I have seen many incredible English rose gardens, but nothing measured up to what I viewed at that moment. Every flower seemed to be *perfectly* in bloom. In this royal display, nothing was out of place. Everything was perfect. The scent of roses filled the air. They looked and smelled spectacular. How fitting that The Queen of the United Kingdom should have such a glorious rose garden to enjoy, and the names of the varieties were fun as well, "Golden Jubilee" and "Gracious Queen," just to name a few.

I could have stayed in the rose garden forever, yet it was time to head back to the main lawn, which by now was filling up with guests. In the background military bands were playing choruses of festive uplifting music, which put everyone in a fun and relaxed mood. Before I knew it, it was time for the tea tent to open.

Approaching the buffet there were grand displays of scones, finger sandwiches, cakes, fruit tarts, profiteroles, and many other delicious offerings. As expected, there were endless amounts of tea and other beverages as well, such as fruit juices from the royal estate at Sandringham.

Perhaps a familiar face amongst the crowd?

While tea itself was quite the affair the real show was about to begin, so I assumed my position - knowing exactly where I needed to stand for the best view of the proceedings.

At 3:55 pm, excitement was in the air, and a hush came over the crowd. And then, at the stroke of 4:00 pm, Her Majesty The Queen and His Royal Highness The Duke of Edinburgh stood at the top of the garden stairs for *God Save The Queen*. I stood at attention while being mindful that I was viewing something very special. After the anthem the royal couple walked down the stairs and stood right in front of me, while a few members of the clergy were presented to them. It was a very warm day and we were in the direct sun for much of the afternoon. Despite the heat, the royal couple looked unflustered as they continued to be presented to countless numbers of people over the next hour. I suspect it was exhausting for them, yet as soon as they reached the Royal Tea Tent I observed that The Queen and Prince Philip turned down the seats offered to them, took a quick sip of their tea, then continued to mingle while standing and meeting other guests.

The entire day was superb for people watching. From the uniforms and hats, to the many types of people and outfits - it was a feast for the eyes. I remember well one lady I spoke with. She had been presented to The Queen and was on cloud nine, glowing with delight at her experience. Other members of the royal family were also in attendance and walked the lawn freely during the event, randomly stopping to chat with guests. This included The Duke of Kent, Princess Alexandra, and The Duchess of Gloucester.

The garden party was drawing to a close. Like many of the best moments, the experience was over in the blink of an eye. It was one of the best afternoons of my life, and as I turned to leave, the military band started to play *When you wish upon a star.*

I stopped, smiled, and thought to myself, "Dreams do come true."

"When you wish upon a star, makes no difference who you are; anything your heart desires, will come to you."

In the gardens of Buckingham Palace, 1 June 2017.

Chapter Nine: Pursuing the Object

Each day Her Majesty The Queen is presented with a handwritten card featuring the Royal Coat of Arms and the words, "The Queen's Engagements." Occasionally these cards are offered for sale, but they tend to be blank, not the ones that are filled out with engagements and their timings.

Imagine my surprise when I discovered buried within an auction lot, a completed, handwritten card for 2 June 1953, the day of The Queen's coronation. The card outlines the departure times from Buckingham Palace, and arrival and departure times at Westminster Abbey, as well as the timings for the flypast and The Queen's radio broadcast that would end the day. My first thought was, how could something this historically significant *not* be housed in the Royal Archives? The engagement card for the most important day of The Queen's reign was a dream for a collector like me. Good provenance is crucial, and this was being sold from the estate of Mr. Ernest Bennett, who had been Page of the Backstairs to The Queen for nearly 30 years.

I sat anxiously in the auction room on the morning of the sale, knowing full-well the importance of the lot described as, "various coronation items." The card was not highlighted in any way within the lot description. It was simply listed amongst various other coronation items - none of which hinted at its importance. Would I be one of the few who noticed it, or would other rival collectors spot this gem as well? It was a nail-biting auction and to my excitement, I won the lot for well under the highest price I was willing to pay for such a piece of history.

Another small example of history can be found in an unexpected, and possibly underestimated piece of cotton wool. Yes, a simple piece of cotton wool. How on earth could that be of historical importance you ask?

Alongside the wool is a note written by the Archbishop of Canterbury at the time. It reads, "Wool used at the anointing of King George VI. Westminster Abbey, May 12, 1937." Both the note and the wool contain traces of the holy oil. This simple piece of cotton was used during the most sacred and intimate part of the coronation service. Before the monarch can receive the symbols of royal authority and be crowned, he or she must be anointed with holy oil. This ritual solidifies his or her role as Supreme Governor of the Church of England.

When it came up for auction I knew I had to have it. It is a bit of a curiosity, but one with profound historical significance. After the coronation the Dean of Westminster presented it to the Bishop of Norwich who was tasked with carrying the bible into the abbey during the procession. Devising a strategy I thought, "How much would someone be willing to pay for a piece of cotton fluff?" Quite a lot, as I soon discovered. The tension mounted as the bids kept going up and up. It took 34 bids, but at last the hammer came down in my favour. Someone later said, "That sure was a lot of fuss for a bit of fluff." Indeed it was, but well worth it still!

Knowledge must be the foundation for building a good collection. Researching your topic on a regular basis, surrounding yourself with others who collect within the same genre, and narrowing your search is vitally important. And every collector makes mistakes. That is all part of building up a base of knowledge and experience. I still kick myself for not making certain purchases, and it is easy to remember the things that got away or things that I simply turned down for various reasons.

One example of note involves a now famous, yet unorthodox signed print of The Queen that was offered to me in 2010 for £1,500 and now changes hands at over £15,000. For me, this is the "big one that got away." Hard lessons such as these make a collector savvier and more sophisticated. "You must know when to jump," as a friend and fellow collector frequently says.

Over the years, I have built up an extensive collection of The Queen's hand-signed letters, notes, cards, and documents, and have become well-versed on the nuances of her hand. During an internet search one evening I came across the site of a stamp dealer in Ohio. Listed was a small handwritten envelope. The description noted that the letter was postmarked from Balmoral Castle, but seeing the photograph I recognised the writing on the envelope as that of Her Majesty The Queen. The envelope was addressed to an artist in Canada who had been commissioned by The Queen from time-to-time in the 1960s. I quickly purchased the envelope for the "hefty" sum of $7.00 USD. In reality, because of what it was, the price should have been in the hundreds.

It all comes back to the importance of knowledge as a collector. For example, the autopen machine (an electronic device that reproduces a signature) was introduced into the royal household around 1960. Many people who believe they own an authentic royal signature are disappointed to discover that the script was written by a machine.

Royal presentation gifts, another area of interest, feature prominently in my collection. They are just as the name suggests - gifts presented, usually in person, by a member of the royal family to the recipient who is sometimes a foreign head of state, an ambassador, or a long-serving member of staff. These gifts include signed photographs, cufflinks, pill boxes, clocks, and stickpins, as well as other objets d'art.

Because there is such variety in the level of items presented, royal presentation gifts are an interesting area to collect. These are popular with aficionados like me, so you must be quick, since there will be others vying for the same objects.

I was with a friend who mentioned that a few days prior he attended an art opening. While there, he noticed an original sketch by royal dressmaker Ian Thomas. It was the design for the ensemble worn by The Queen to the wedding of Prince Charles and Lady Diana Spencer in 1981. He mentioned the name of the seller and said, "It would be perfect for your collection." Indeed it would! I knew I had to be quick and spring into action. Something that rare would not go unsold for long.

The next morning I spoke with the seller and immediately jumped onto a train and made my way to his studio in Essex. Later that day I returned to London with the sketch in hand, as well as a few other drawings of dresses designed for The Queen. These were sketches of dresses that I didn't recognise, so it was time for the research to commence.

First, the internet, but no luck. Then it was time to go through my own library, page by page. In my search to match the sketches with the dresses, I looked through hundreds of photographs. Eventually, I managed to locate images of the dresses featured in the sketches. One was an aquamarine dress worn by Her Majesty aboard the *Royal Yacht Britannia*. In the photograph she is pictured alongside President and Mrs. Reagan, and The Duke of Edinburgh.

Previously I shared my interest in artistry and craftsmanship, and what goes into the making of objects. Whether it is a piece of silver by Gerald Benney or Stuart Devlin, or a hand-painted enamel box by Halcyon Days, like many other aspects of my life this interest in fine craftsmanship started at a young age.

Throughout my childhood there were English enamel boxes dotted around the house. They were always there, yet over time I became enamoured by them. Hand-painted, many with quotations or reminders of special occasions. I knew they were special to my mother for sentimental reasons.

At the age of 16, I saved up to purchase my first Halcyon Days Enamel box for $125.00 USD, which was a large amount of money for a teenager. It arrived "all the way from England" and I still remember the pride I felt when admiring it and showing it off to others. While other 16-year olds were saving to buy a car, my interests were clearly in another world. I still have that enamel box to this day, along with 400 others! Minimalism has never been my strong suit.

Who needs minimalism?

Once you have acquired the objects, long-term conservation is vitally important. Damages from UV light, changes in temperatures and humidity, and archival storage, in addition to security and insurance are things that must be considered. Limiting direct sunlight, using UV protective film on exterior windows, as well as framing with acid free mounts and museum glass, ensures that the objects will endure the test of time.

Restoration is another important consideration for a collector and can be rewarding. Finding someone with the knowledge and sensitivity to take an object that has been "well used" over the years and restore it to its original splendour can be challenging. I had a great working relationship with Guy Davis, a talented conservator based in Indianapolis, and we worked on many projects together. I knew that regardless of the scruffy, worn, or damaged state of the object I could take it to Guy and he would have it looking better than new at the end of the day.

While in a favourite shop in Yorkshire I noticed an exquisite hand painted object. The retail price was £1,750, yet I spotted a small chip that had gone unnoticed by the staff. I pointed out the damage and in despair they admitted that the item would be a write off. I knew that thousands of miles away Guy could make it "perfect again." Knowing it was likely an insurance loss, the shopkeeper sold it to me for £150.00. A few weeks later in Indianapolis, I took it to Guy knowing the magic he could perform. He fully restored it for $150.00 USD, and I would challenge anyone today to notice that it had ever been damaged. The lesson? Never underestimate the skills of a good restorer!

The pursuit and preservation of objects is one thing, but displaying and sharing them is the best part of all. For years I maintained a residence in Indianapolis, and after every excursion to the UK my home there became more and more full of objects. I would fly to Britain with a small suitcase fitted within a large empty suitcase, then the large one would return to the US filled with acquisitions. This continued for years.

My last home in Indianapolis was a former Victorian school building with high ceilings and many original features. It was the perfect setting to serve as a backdrop for my collection. Over the years, my "Britain in miniature" was featured during local television programmes on several occasions. As a collector the highlight was seeing my home featured in an eight-page spread in *Indianapolis Monthly* titled, "House of Windsor."

This was a play on words, known only to myself and to the journalist, since my home was situated in the Windsor Park neighbourhood of Indianapolis. As time went on I was spending less and less time in Indianapolis, or even in the US. Transcendent Travel had taken off, and my life was becoming more and more grounded in the United Kingdom. I was never happier than when I was in the UK, and the back and forth travel to the states became exhausting and seemed pointless. I would often arrive back in the US wondering, "Why am I doing this?" I had friends there, but my life had moved on, as had theirs.

It was time to make a change. All of my life had been a pursuit of Britain.

It was time to move the collection and myself from Windsor Park to Windsor, England.

Chapter Ten:
Windsor Park to Windsor

The decision to move and live in Britain full-time was an easy one. It had been years in the making and represented the culmination of a dream. In every way, Britain agreed with me. The way of life, the culture, and the rich, vibrant history all made my soul sing in a way that I had never experienced on the other side of the Atlantic. When I was in my 20s, I would often think, "Who do I need to work for in order to live in England?" Years later I finally answered that question. Myself.

This is not to say that it was easy to gather my belongings and move to Britain - quite the opposite. It took years of building a business followed by endless paperwork, red tape, and immigration lawyers in order to be able to legally come to work and later live in Britain. My business partner Kathryn was instrumental in moving this monotonous process along, a job not to be underestimated.

Before I decided to move my collection to the UK, I had to obtain a work visa as well as a residence permit. With that part of the process completed it was time for the next stage, obtaining a full transfer of residency, making it possible to ship my belongings, and most importantly, my collection. This was a lengthy and arduous process that required jumping through multiple hoops.

The logistics of any move can be complicated at the best of times. An international move is all of that and more, especially when moving large furniture, art, and 600 books, as well as thousands of objects - most of which are fragile. Where would I choose to live?

After much consideration it was obvious that I needed to live in a place that spoke to my passion for all things royal. Surprise, surprise, where else but Windsor! Its close proximity to London, while still being near the countryside and a quick commute to Heathrow were desirable features. A residence in Windsor would afford me the opportunity to go home between the many weeks of tours during the summer. What a difference it would make to someone who lives out of a suitcase for months on end.

Now, who could I trust to move my collection across the country and overseas? The research commenced. In the end I selected an international moving company based in Chicago. Their claim to fame, they specialised in international art and antique removals. They were perfect for the big job ahead.

My first video call with the company was several months prior to the actual moving date. I would love to know what went through their minds as I showed them the multitude of objects, since so many pertained to the British royal family. The walls were lined with pictures, there were flags and banners hanging from the high ceilings, the closets were full, and in addition the kitchen cupboards were filled with royal memorabilia instead of pots and pans. The collection had overtaken almost *every single inch* of my home.

They were stunned, and it didn't take long before they stated that it would require an entire LARGE shipping container. Hiring a company whose professionalism is highly rated also comes with a high price tag. After the quote finally settled in I signed the agreement, and put the decision to bed for a few months. I had to prepare for six months of tours.

Once my tours ended my thoughts returned to the big move. Over several days I worked with three people, meticulously wrapping as many items as we could by hand. This work was merely in preparation, since when the day arrived five professional movers spent twelve hours carefully wrapping the remainder of the collection. One hilarious moment happened when a mover stopped everything. He could hear a noise coming from one of the sealed boxes he had just picked up. I said dryly, "Oh, don't worry. It's just playing *God Save The Queen*." We all laughed.

The tally kept going up, and up, and up - 198 boxes of all sizes - huge, medium, enormous, and small. Oh, and there was furniture as well. Some items even had to go into custom-made wooden crates. It required three insurance companies for the move: one in the United States, one at sea, and one upon arrival to the United Kingdom. I watched like a hawk as my treasures were wrapped for their long voyage to Britain. It had been a mentally exhausting experience, and as the truck pulled away I felt a sense of relief. Although I would not see my things for over a month, at least the first part of the ordeal was over.

The collection headed off to Chicago where the boxes and crates were packed into the shipping container. The container then travelled via train to New York and was loaded onto a ship for the journey overseas. So many steps, but there was irony in the experience. These objects had made this journey already - one by one over the years. A friend said it best, "Your collection is coming home."

About to board the Queen Mary 2 in New York.

Some objects were too special to have out of my sight. I drove these to New York City and travelled to England with them on the *Queen Mary 2*. Never one to turn down the opportunity to make a memory, I choose travel by ocean liner. I wanted my arrival to England to be done in a special way, the way that so many had emigrated in the past. Luckily this transatlantic voyage was smooth and we didn't experience rough seas, unlike prior crossings. The peaceful six-day journey across the Atlantic allowed me the chance to decompress from the first part of the move. It was also an opportunity to contemplate the future.

I found myself in a very reflective mood as the ship sailed out of New York harbour. I was turning the page. Standing on deck with a glass of champagne in hand, I toasted the Statue of Liberty and looked to the east - towards my future life. It had taken years to achieve this dream, and when I arrived at Southampton I knew it represented a new and exciting chapter.

Raising a glass to the Statue of Liberty as I sailed for Britain.

A few weeks later the day came for my container to arrive. My new neighbours got quite a surprise as this huge monstrosity pulled up in front of my home. Up close, a full-size shipping container is *enormous*. It felt as if it was larger than the house. As my friend Karen Mangia said so cleverly at the time, "Andrew, that's the ugliest and most expensive box you've ever purchased." Indeed it was!

As the movers carried in all 198 boxes, as well as the furniture, the arduous chore of unpacking commenced. It took the next couple of months to fully unpack and display my collection. Amazingly, only one item had been broken during the journey. It was a glass shelf which was easily replaced. In the end the movers came through with their packing efforts.

After settling into my new home the time came to begin planning my tours for 2020. Or so I thought.

Life is not always "smooth sailing", as the world would discover during the pandemic of 2020. Like so many others, I experienced a roller coaster year, not without difficulties and challenges.

Now in Windsor, my months were spent cancelling arrangements I had already made for tours, while watching guests cancel or postpone the journeys they had booked with us. For someone who tries very hard to be an optimist the future looked grim. I experienced the age-old, "you don't know what you have until it's gone."

In challenging times like these I find myself reflecting back to the tour guest who said, "Thank you Andrew, for giving me one of the best weeks of my life." Memories like these make me realise that creating memorable moments for others are when I am at my happiest and living *my* best life.

If the pandemic has taught me anything, it has taught me not to take things for granted, to accept the bad days and cherish the good days. For they all come into our lives for a reason. One of my favourite songs is titled *Here's to Life*. In many ways it sums up my attitude toward living when it says, "May all your storms be weathered. And all that's good get better." While this song has been a favourite of mine for years, I now understand and appreciate the poignant lyrics much more.

How appropriate that I write these final words on the 72nd Wedding Anniversary of The Queen and The Duke of Edinburgh. On the day they were married Britain was still recovering from the wounds of the Second World War. Their wedding was celebrated with hope and optimism for the future, and Prime Minister Winston Churchill described it as, "A flash of colour on the hard road we travel." After 1947, peace and prosperity flourished again. Today, their wedding anniversary reminds me, once again, that life does go on.

I look forward to the next chapter of the journey. You can bet it will involve more travelling, collecting, and royal adventures and I'll keep sharing my passion for these with others. I have found that to be the most rewarding part of all. The song goes on,

> *"No complaints and no regrets*
> *I still believe in chasing dreams and placing bets*
> *For I have learned that all you give is all you get*
> *So give it all you've got*
> *I had my share, I drank my fill*
> *And even though I'm satisfied, I'm hungry still*
> *To see what's down another road, beyond the hill*
> *And do it all again*
> *So, here's to life and all the joy it brings*
> *Yes, here's to life and dreamers and their dreams."*

- Here's to Life written by Phyllis Molinary & Artie Butler

As I reflect on my adventures thus far - some royal, some exotic, some challenging and some hilarious - I smile as I think back to that young boy in Indiana, combing over maps and collecting his travel brochures. Dreaming of the places he hoped to see.

While unpacking a random box after the move I stumbled across a small, framed image of Windsor Castle. Forgetting I even had it, I turned it over. Seeing the label attached I suddenly realised that I bought it when I was only 15 years old.

I'd like to whisper to that young man, "Keep perusing your passions, for they will take you even further than you can imagine."

That advice has been true for me. May it be so for all of us.

***

Acknowledgments

I would like to thank my business partner Kathryn Rice for her support in achieving not only my professional dreams, but my personal ones as well.

Thank you to Elaine Klemesrud who steadfastly supports me, as well as our clients in a professional and cheerful way. You were *instrumental* in the completion of this book. I cannot thank you enough for your time, patience, and guidance.

When you have friends that are also authors the process of writing a book is not as daunting, and for that I must thank Karen Mangia who inspires me and keeps me laughing.

I must also acknowledge Kimberly Blakeley, Penny & Jamie Neilson, Eric Stark, Michael Pettry, Richard Miles, Stephanie Collins, Dan Hamby, and Tina Waganer. The parts you have each played in my story are greatly appreciated and are not forgotten.

My thanks go to Declan Morton for his consultation and editing of the manuscript, and to Stephanie Derybowski for her talented designs and the ability to read my mind on frequent occasions.

My gratitude also goes to Ken Man for his steadfast support and for listening to me talking about this project for many months on end. 2020 was a much better year because of you.

Thank you to my many past and present tour guests, for without you the journey would not have been as enriching and the story could not have come this far.

And finally, with special thanks to my darling friend Rosanna Hardin Hall for planting the seed in 2012 that I needed to write a book. Your persistence did the trick. I am proud to call you my friend.

Printed in Great Britain
by Amazon